Get That Te

A companion website to accompany this book is available online at:

http://education.ainsworth.continuumbooks.com

Please type in the URL above and receive your unique password for access to the book's online resources.

If you experience any problems accessing the resources, please contact Continuum at: info@continuumbooks.com

Also available from Continuum

Developing a Self-Evaluating School, Paul K. Ainsworth
Not Quite a Teacher, Tom Bennett
The Ultimate Teaching Manual, Gererd Dixie

Get That Teaching Job!

PAUL K. AINSWORTH

continuum

Continuum International Publishing Group

The Tower Building	80 Maiden Lane
11 York Road	Suite 704
London	New York
SE1 7NX	NY 10038

www.continuumbooks.com

British Library Cataloguing-in-Publication Data
A catalogue record for this book is available from the British Library.

ISBN: 978-1-4411-1332-0 (paperback)

Library of Congress Cataloging-in-Publication Data
Ainsworth, Paul, 1973-
  Get that teaching job! / Paul K. Ainsworth.
        p. cm.
  Includes bibliographical references and index.
  ISBN 978-1-4411-1332-0 (pbk. : alk. paper) -- ISBN 978-1-4411-4522-2 (ebook epub : alk. paper) -- ISBN 978-1-4411-7897-8 (ebook pdf : alk. paper) 1. Teachers--Employment--Great Britain--Handbooks, manuals, etc. 2. Job hunting--Great Britain--Handbooks, manuals, etc. 3. Teaching--Vocational guidance--Great Britain--Handbooks, manuals, etc. I. Title.
  LB1780.A47 2012
  371.102'341--dc23
            2011022994

Typeset by Fakenham Prepress Solutions, Fakenham, Norfolk NR21 8NN
Printed and bound in India

To my family, C, J and S for all your support especially with my mad cap job ideas.

Contents

Acknowledgements

Thank you to R, who as a recruitment consultant gave me such great advice so many years ago and to J for taking the risk in supporting my career.

I would like to thank D, an RAF officer who taught me how to prepare for job interviews whether for Initial Officer Training or for a teaching job in such a strategic manner.

I would also like to thank all those colleagues who have been prepared to share their wonderful applications with me and allowed me to use sections of them in the letters in this book. Particular thanks go to Fiona, Becky, Julia, Emily and Kate.

I also wish to thank my colleagues at Belvoir High School alongside whom I have made many appointments, in particular H for keeping me so organized.

Finally I would like to thank the many colleagues at Continuum Press who have worked so hard turning my manuscript into the final book.

Wherever you see this symbol, go to the companion website to download templates for CVs, letters of application, and other resources to help you to prepare for your interview.

How to use this book

Get That Teaching Job! has been written so it can be read in different ways according to your experience and your needs as a job hunter. You may be beginning the process of applying for jobs and so choose to read this book in a linear fashion from beginning to end: as a result you will build up a full and practical knowledge of how you can develop your job application technique. Or you may have seen a particular job advertisement this week and want advice on how to structure a strong application. You could be in the even better position of having an interview offer for next week and wish to concentrate on honing your interview technique or building your confidence. Perhaps you have a specific concern which has been raised in an interview debrief; this book will help you to address all these issues.

Following the introduction the book is divided into three distinct sections. The first of these (pages 11 to 88) gives advice on the different stages in the process involved in obtaining a teaching job, from choosing the right type of school for you, through structuring and strengthening your application and preparing for and handling the interview itself. The second section (pages 89 to 146) gives **advice specific to certain roles**. The final section (pages 147 to 166) considers your **reflection process** after an interview and how, if or when necessary, you can ensure you are an even stronger candidate next time.

If you do not want to read the book from cover to cover, why not read the introduction? You can dip into chapters which immediately take your interest. Each chapter has been divided into three sections:

◆ the basics
◆ the detail
◆ final thoughts.

If you just wish to gain an outline of the chapter and briefly consider if you need to study further, read 'the basics'. The set of questions at the end of these sections will help you relate these initial paragraphs to your own situation and decide if you want to read 'the detail' or move straight onto the next chapter. Within 'the detail' you will find detailed advice about the topic of the chapter. The 'final thoughts' section revisits what you need to know and includes a set of questions enabling you to reflect on the chapter.

Student teachers

You may feel considerable pressure as you begin applying for teaching jobs after spending four years studying and accumulating debt. You may have watched your peers with other degrees having already had a year's worth of pay packets with all the benefits that brings. You may also have a limited number of people to ask for advice and your fellow student teachers will have had few learning experiences themselves.

It is important that when you arrive for an interview you have some idea of what to expect. You do not want to spend your first interview feeling out of your depth. Take your time to read this book and reflect on the advice that is given. It is a good idea to read it over a period of time and make notes on the sections that seem important to you. Then when you see a job advert that you wish to apply for return to the sections in the book that help with this and do the same when you are called for interview. If things do not go according to plan, it is important to learn from the experience and this book can help you do that by reflecting on what went wrong or what you could have done to present yourself in a better light.

Main scale teachers

It may be that this is the time in your career when you need to make a change as you are starting to feel a little bit stale in your first job. You may also need a new job for personal reasons; perhaps you want to shorten your commute or move schools so that you are closer to your partner. Or you may have seen an advert for a school that you have always dreamed of.

At this stage in your career you are likely to be far more selective with your applications and hence really want to make sure that any letters you write or interviews you attend show you at your best. In such circumstances you may wish to dip into the chapters that feel most appropriate at the time to you.

Middle leaders

Many teachers wish to apply for a middle leadership post at some stage in their career. There is no doubt that application procedures for middle leadership posts are different from those for main scale posts. Some middle leadership posts can be very competitive indeed with a large number of applicants, whereas you may find a post such as Head of Mathematics attracts few applicants. The pressures are very different as a result. However, it is important to remember that at middle leadership level school leaders will be prepared not to appoint if there if there is no-one suitable.

Common feedback for middle leader applicants is that they have not understood the difference between applying for a leadership role and a main scale teaching one. Careful reading of the appropriate sections of this book will ensure that you do not receive this feedback.

It is common for there to be internal applications for middle leadership posts. If you are an internal candidate, senior leaders will be expecting you to have made a step up from the answers you gave as a main scale teacher and this book will help you to make that progression.

Once you have attained the role of a middle leader it is likely that you will be expected to participate in the interview process on the other side of the fence. Your Headteacher may even ask you to write the list of interview questions or structure the day. The primary aim of this book is not to teach you how to conduct interviews but rather to offer useful suggestions for interview questions, ideas for interview tasks, or advice on how to structure an interview. You will also be seen by your Head as presenting fresh ideas to your school.

Senior leaders

The world of senior leadership posts is completely different from the other interviews. Senior leaders and governors will be expecting a great deal from candidates and you will also find that you will be competing against very talented individuals. The maxim of 'failing to prepare is preparing to fail' is never truer than at this level. You need to reflect seriously on your strengths as a middle leader when you are applying for senior leadership posts and carefully consider how these talents will aid a school at senior leadership level.

This book will help you sharpen your game to make sure you project yourself at your very best and continue to progress your career in the way that you wish.

End note

Few people enjoy the process of job application but the feeling of elation that comes from being offered a job that you really dreamt of will stay with you for a long time. I hope that you do not let this book become dusty on a shelf, but instead scribble your thoughts in the margin and return to its pages throughout your teaching career.

Introduction

There is no doubt that one of the keys to being happy as a teacher is to find the right school to work in. Some teachers seem to change schools almost every year and equally in almost every staff room there are colleagues who have happily spent their entire career at that one school. I can remember one colleague who had started at a school as a PGCE student and then 30 years later had become Principal of the school. Not every teacher wishes to become a Principal or Headteacher but every teacher wants to find the location where they can build their career, extend their skills and feel part of a community.

At every point in your career there will be a particular job that you really want. It may be that you have just finished your Initial Teacher Training and a role is advertised which you feel is a perfect starting point. You may wish to move to a new location for personal reasons and a job appears at a school that would suit your background. It may be that you have an ambition to work in a particular type of school. Or you may even be a teacher looking at a senior leadership post at a school which you have visited before and have since wished you could work at.

When the advertisement for such a job appears there is pressure to construct a strong application and then, if selected, perform to your full potential on the day or even days of interview. There is considerable competition on such days and other candidates will be preparing as much as possible. In addition, teachers often recognize that they have only one chance to really shine, since if they do not gain the role it may never appear again or they may feel that they cannot go back to the school for a second chance. Therefore it is important to try to discount the other applicants for the role and try to ensure you give the interviewers as much positive information as possible about yourself and why you particularly suit the role in order to secure it.

For many senior leaders and middle leaders, interviewing for a new teacher post can be one of the most exciting points of the year as there is the optimism of hopefully bringing in a new teacher who could really make the difference. Yet it is often frustrating to receive applications that are badly written or when applicants present themselves poorly at interview.

The aim of this book is to ensure that you, as an applicant, can show your potential school what you are really capable of. There will be lots of advice on how you can perfect your application so that it stands out from the crowd and gets you through to the interview stage. The second stage of this book will help you to polish your technique so that you are undaunted by the competitive environment of the interview. It is not about getting you a job that you are not suited to but it will give you an advantage the next time that you see a role advertised and think 'that's the post for me!'

Changes in recruitment practice

If you are in initial training one of your queries will be 'how do schools interview?' and if you have not applied for a job recently you may wonder if the process has changed. If you talk to more senior members of the staffroom you will note considerable changes in recruitment practice. Thirty years ago, teachers did not usually apply to individual schools but rather to a Local Authority (LA). You would have been interviewed by an LA employee at County Hall and never visited a school or seen a child. These were known as pool interviews. If you were successful you would then be allocated to a specific school which you had never even visited.

Until 20 years ago, the quality of your handwriting would have been crucial to your success in getting to an interview, as application forms and letters had to be written by hand. This is very different from today, where the whole process of application can take place via the internet without any physical contact with the school.

In the last 15 years it has become commonplace for teachers to have to deliver a lesson as part of the interview process. This is often a nerve-wracking part of the process but very sensible as, after all, you are being paid to teach. In addition it gives you an opportunity to try to discover whether your methods will be suited to the school you have applied to.

In recent years there has been a rise in the involvement of pupils in the interview process. They may take you on tours around the school or interview you themselves. In some schools they have been trained to observe teachers teach or be part of the final interview panel.

It is interesting to consider how teaching interviews could be developed in the future. Will there be a rise in on-line testing to help shortlist candidates and a reduction in the written application part of the process? Perhaps teachers' ICT skills will be tested more specifically as it is almost expected nowadays that teachers are skilled in the use of interactive whiteboards and virtual learning environments.

The current job market

Another of your concerns will be 'how many jobs are out there?' The current job market for teachers is not as rosy as it has been in the past. Equally there is also considerable polarization in the availability of teachers for certain roles. In the last decade it has always been a challenge for Newly Qualified Teachers to gain a job in a good primary school. Primary Headteachers will often talk of receiving 50+ applications for such a main scale post particularly in an area where there is a strong presence from teacher training establishments. Yet there may be very few applications for Primary Headteacher posts particularly in small rural primary schools.

At secondary level in some metropolitan cities there will be very few applicants for main scale posts. Nationwide, Headteachers will talk about the gold dust of a Physics teacher or maybe a Head of Mathematics. Yet for other secondary school posts there can be large numbers of applicants for such roles as Physical Education (PE) teacher. This situation is likely to be exacerbated by the uncertainty within the school sports partnerships.

In the foreseeable future, owing to the current economic situation, school budgets will have to be squeezed. For an average school, over 80 per cent of the budget is spent on staffing so that is the most obvious place to make savings. Schools will be resistant to making redundancies but they may reduce the number of non-contact lessons that teachers have with the aim of not replacing teachers if they leave. Another opportunity for savings is to reduce the number of middle and senior leadership posts by the creation of flatter staffing structures, i.e. where there are fewer levels in the school's leadership hierarchy: perhaps Department Heads instead of Faculty Heads, line managed by senior leaders. Another example of a flatter management structure is where there are fewer senior leaders, e.g. in some schools there are no Deputy Heads but a senior team consisting of Assistant

Heads and the Headteacher. There has also been an increase in collaborations between schools which can be used to reduce the number of senior leadership posts and hence save money in that way.

In many areas of the country, schools have surplus places and local authorities are under pressure from government to consider rationalization, i.e. close or amalgamate schools, which again can lead to fewer teachers being required.

Due to the economic downturn many people have lost jobs in the private sector and graduates have also found that private sector companies have reduced their recruitment. This has meant there has been an increase in the number of people beginning initial teacher training routes, whether in Higher Education such as PGCE courses or through in-school training routes such as the Graduate Training Programme. The current government has also announced plans to make it easier for members of the armed forces to become teachers or for other graduates to have fast track routes into teaching, mirroring the Teach First scheme from the United States. It is also inevitable that students beginning Higher Education are more attracted to courses that have obvious employment routes, including degrees which result in qualified teacher status.

All these factors indicate that the job market will become ever more competitive. There will always be jobs in schools that are struggling or in parts of the country where there is a high cost of living. However, in my experience entrants to the profession who begin working in such locations are those who are either the most likely to leave the profession or to find less personal fulfilment from their roles. There will be always be exceptions to such blanket statements and some of the highest calibre teachers are those with an immense personal commitment to the profession which ensures that in such an environment they thrive and do make a significant difference to the lives of the young people they work with. They are also likely to make rapid progress in their careers at the same time.

Reasons for confidence

You may feel after reading about the current job market that all your fears have foundation and that you are sentenced to a life of toil as a supply teacher or moving from one short-term contract to another – even if you are lucky enough to gain such roles.

This is not the case at all. The first reason for confidence is that you are already thinking about how you can be a stronger applicant for a post. There will be many teachers who consider that there is nothing they can do to improve their chances. They feel helpless that their performance in their career so far or other choices that they have made decide their future. This is not the case. You can always improve your chances and just thinking about how you can do so already puts you at an advantage.

The second reason is your investment in this book. You are obviously prepared to act and make changes to your applications. I read countless applications and am continually frustrated that some people have wasted time sending an application with hardly any thought given to it and yet still expect an interviewer to read it. There are a few little tricks that this book will suggest which should make a difference because so few applicants use them.

Third, in the commercial world graduates spend time working on their interview technique and practising questions and as a result feel more confident and able to project their natural personality on the day. It is apparent from conversations with senior leaders from other professions that many teaching applicants do not carry out sufficient research and are therefore disappointed. Those applicants who have prepared thoroughly for their interview stand head and shoulders above the rest.

Lastly, you need to remember that interviewers *want* applicants to shine. In the world of education, senior leaders *want* to have a difficult choice because the candidates have interviewed so well and are usually secretly willing you to perform to your best, however professionally distant they may appear.

With some careful thought and reflection, both on the material in this book and on your previous interview performances, and then putting the resulting ideas into practice you will find that you are more confident. You will then be more at ease at interview and more able to show the interviewers what you can offer their school.

Get That Teaching Job!

Get That Teaching Job! is divided into three sections. The first section considers general advice to job hunters which is not specific to a particular role. Section Two gives advice which is focused on applying for certain roles. The third and final section considers how applicants can reflect on an unsuccessful experience and gives more advanced guidance. Further details of how the book is structured and the guidance it provides are given below:

Section One: General Advice for Job Hunters

Chapter 1: What type of school do you wish to work in? (Pages 13 to 22)

There is a huge variety in the type of schools which teachers can currently work in. There are the obvious sectors of primary and secondary schools and then the maintained and independent sectors. There has been a growth in the different types of state schools including Local Authority schools, Voluntary Aided and Voluntary Controlled schools, Trust and Foundation schools, Academies and the new Free schools. It is important that when you are applying to a school you consider what impact the different status will have on your working life.

This chapter includes guidance on:

◆ comparing the different types of school
◆ how different types of school will affect your terms and conditions.

Chapter 2: Where to look for jobs (pages 23 to 28)

Many teachers will be under the impression that all teaching jobs must be advertised in *The Times Educational Supplement* and will focus their efforts on this publication and its website. However, the reality is that there are many other avenues to explore for job vacancies and if you only focus on one source it is likely that you will miss some opportunities that could be perfect for you.

This chapter includes guidance on:

◆ periodicals where jobs are advertised
◆ using the internet to find teaching jobs.

Chapter 3: How to structure your written application (pages 29 to 42)

The first view a school will have of you is your written application, whether this is a letter of application, an application form or a curriculum vitae (CV). A strong application will never get you a job but it gets you to the interview and possibly to the front of the pack. It is therefore surprising how many teachers get their written application so badly wrong.

This chapter includes guidance and advice on:

◆ the different types of CV which can be used
◆ the golden rules on constructing a letter of application

◆ how a carefully completed application form can support your letter.

Chapter 4: How strong is your application? (Pages 43 to 52)

All candidates will wish to be able to assess how suitable they are for a particular position and then how strong their application is. This chapter will give you the skills to analyse your own skills and gauge whether this post is one worth applying for.

This chapter includes guidance on:

◆ will the school consider my application?
◆ will there be people better qualified than me?

Chapter 5: What interview tasks could you face? (Pages 53 to 64)

Once you have developed a winning application format which communicates your strong skills you should begin to receive invitations to attend interviews. In addition to a standard interview, schools have begun to use a wide variety of tasks to choose the successful candidate from teaching a lesson to completing a role play. This chapter considers a selection of interview tasks which you may be asked to participate in.

The chapter includes guidance on:

◆ the range of tasks that may be used during selection day/s
◆ what the interviewer may be looking for from the candidates
◆ how you can present your strengths effectively.

Chapter 6: How to prepare for your interview (pages 65 to 74)

The previous chapter considered the variety of tasks that may be used by schools to differentiate applicants but often the final decision will be based on a formal interview often with the Headteacher or another senior leader, a governor and a second member of the school staff. This chapter considers techniques that you can use to prepare for interviews and how you can structure your answers.

The chapter includes guidance on:

◆ how you can prepare for interviews
◆ how you can structure your answers.

Chapter 7: A general guide to interviews (pages 75 to 82)

Those teachers who have attended interviews will often say the questions are completely different from school to school, and other teachers may say there is a huge difference between the questions that a newly qualified teacher (NQT) will be asked in comparison to those posed to a Headteacher candidate. However, when you analyse teaching interviews you will find there is a set of core questions that will often be asked and a similar structure used.

The chapter includes guidance on:

◆ how an interview may be structured
◆ the general interview questions that will be asked
◆ how you can tackle these questions.

Chapter 8: How to present yourself (pages 83 to 88)
As an interviewer it is fascinating to look at the different ways that candidates present themselves in an interview scenario. Research has been done on how effective this is in increasing your interview success. In schools often the first person you will meet is the school receptionist, who will make a judgement on who is the best candidate almost purely from their body language and it is surprising how often the candidate they pick is the one who is appointed.

The chapter includes guidance on:

◆ how to make a strong first impression
◆ your general appearance
◆ how you can practise your body language.

Section Two: Choosing the Position for You

In Section Two there are three chapters which give specific advice for teachers looking to obtain roles of differing seniority. Many teachers get stuck at a certain point in a school hierarchy and part of the reason for this can be that they do not understand how the interview requirements change for different positions.

Each chapter will include guidance on:

◆ structuring your CV
◆ writing your letter of application
◆ answering specific interview questions related to the role.

The chapters in Section Two are:

Chapter 9: Becoming a classroom teacher (pages 91 to 108)

Chapter 10: Becoming a middle leader (pages 109 to 126)

Chapter 11: Becoming a senior leader (pages 127 to 146)

Section Three: Reflecting on Your Application and Interview

Chapter 12: Learning from feedback (pages 149 to 154)
Whether you are successful or not, in the interview stage of the process it is important that you learn from the process. There are many advisors who suggest you need to apply for a job before the one you really want appears, so that you have the opportunity to test yourself in an interview environment and present yourself to people you have not previously met.

This chapter will include guidance on:

◆ asking for feedback on your application
◆ receiving feedback on your interview performance
◆ learning from your experience for future interviews.

Chapter 13: Making best use of supply work (pages 155 to 160)
In the current climate as a newly qualified teacher you may not be able to immediately find employment in a full-time permanent post. You may be a more experienced teacher who has left a permanent position. In these situations you may find that you have to take temporary supply positions or short-term contracts.

This chapter will include guidance on:

◆ different types of supply work
◆ contacting schools directly
◆ working with supply agencies.

Chapter 14: The power of networking (pages 161 to 166)
If you are really determined to get a position in a certain type of school which you do not have the appropriate experience for you may need to take a longer term view and plan strategically how you can increase your chances. Ideas and techniques to raise your profile

are more commonplace in the world of business but can be equally effective in education.

This chapter includes guidance on:

◆ understanding networks
◆ building your network.

End note

Trying to find that elusive job is not always an easy process. Some people can be appointed to the first job they apply for whereas other teachers, particularly if they are looking for senior leadership posts in a certain sector of education, can apply for 50 posts before they are successful. However, there is no doubt that all applicants can increase their chances of success by carefully considering how they present themselves in person and by letter.

Section One: General Advice for Job Hunters

1 | What type of school do you wish to work in?

The basics

The vast range of different types of school which has been created in recent years could confuse many job hunters – even those not new to the profession. If you are looking for your first job you need to be aware of how the terms and conditions will vary in different types of school and if this could impact upon your future career. The same will also be true if you are an experienced teacher as there may be things that you currently take for granted that may not be available in a different type of school. In addition, at middle or senior leadership level you may be asked why you wish to work in the type of school you are applying for and it is important that you have a clear answer.

There will be some choices that will already have been made for you due to the training you have undertaken. The most obvious example of this is whether you have qualified in primary or secondary education. Even though it is possible to move between the two sectors, it is not easy to transfer the skills and knowledge. There is a blurring in certain areas of the country with middle schools in the state sector or with some preparatory schools. The other main distinction is between state-funded education, otherwise known as the maintained sector, and the independent sector or private sector.

In this chapter the different schools will be briefly considered, focusing on the impact this will have on you as a teacher.

Identifying your starting point

- What type of school are you qualified to work in?
- Is there a particular type of school you wish to work in?
- What will be the effect of this choice?
- Do you wish to change to a different type of school?
- What impact will this have on you?

The detail

The major division in schools in this country is between the state and independent sectors. The following table seeks to establish the major differences.

Table 1.1: Differences between state and independent sector schools

Factor	State	Independent Sector
Age range of pupils	Most primary schools have the structure 4–11 but there are also some infant schools and junior schools. Most secondary schools are 11–16 or 11–18 but this may change if there are middle schools. In some areas of the country there are middle schools which have various structures 8–13, 9–13, 10–14 or 11–14.	As with middle schools there is a huge range of preparatory school (prep) structures ranging from 3–13 to 8–13. There are also pre-preparatory (pre-prep) schools which tend to cover the 3–7 age range. There are many through independent schools which have the age range 3–18. These tend to be divided into three sections: pre-prep, prep and the senior school. There are secondary schools with an 11–16, 11–18 and in some situations a 13–18 age range.
Salary	Set according by a national bargaining structure. There are three categories; inner London, London fringe and national schools can set their own scales for middle leadership and senior leadership posts.	Each school sets its own pay scale; many choose to follow the state sector for main scale posts sometimes with an additional allowance. At middle and senior leadership level there can be huge variation, with some Independent schools paying much less than state sector schools and some paying much more.

Factor	State	Independent Sector
Additional benefits	Some schools will provide financial support for further qualifications, relocation costs and in some rare instances private medical care!	Dependents may get reduced school fees but this can vary hugely from no fees payable up to a 30 per cent reduction. There can be financial support for further qualifications, relocation costs and medical care. Accommodation may be provided free of charge or at a subsidized rate especially in boarding schools.
Pension	All teachers are members of the Teachers' Pension Scheme and schools contribute.	Most schools are members of the Teachers' Pension Scheme but not all.
Holidays	Pupils attend school for 190 days a year. There is a maximum of five teacher days which can be placed during the year.	Pupils in independent schools usually attend for fewer days than in the state sector and have longer holidays. This is determined by each school.

Factor	State	Independent Sector
Hours of work	Teachers are contracted to work 1265 directed hours. This includes the 190 days, the five teacher days and other meetings which the school can determine. On the senior leadership scale, staff are expected to work reasonable hours at the discretion of the Headteacher.	The school day will often be longer and in some independent schools there will be Saturday school with lessons in the morning and sports fixtures in the afternoon to which all teachers are expected to contribute. Teachers may have to supervise late study on a rota and where there is no Saturday school, teachers may have to complete a rota day once a term. This is where you may have to supervise boarding children or a detention on one Saturday in the term. At senior leadership level hours may be longer with staff expected in school during the holiday period.
Non-contact time	All teachers have 10 per cent of their week as non-contact time. Schools can only 'rarely' call upon teachers to use this time to cover for absent colleagues. There will be significant variation between the quantity of non-contact time given to middle and senior leaders.	There is no set amount of non-contact time and there can be huge variation among schools. Teachers are expected to cover for absent colleagues in most circumstances. There is a tradition that the amount of non-contact time is less in the Independent sector, right up to Headteacher level in secondary schools where it would be more common for an independent school Head to teach than in the state sector.

Factor	State	Independent Sector
Class size	State schools try to keep class sizes under 30 but this will vary according to the demographics in primary and the ability of the children in secondary school.	Independent schools make a huge play of their smaller class sizes and it is very rare to find classes above 20 pupils.
Continuous service for maternity, paternity and sick benefits	In the state sector if you move between schools your service is continuous. Some schools will also include a move from independent to state, meaning you retain your benefits.	Strictly speaking, if you move to an independent school they may not honour your continuous service in terms of benefits. Different schools take different views.

There is a blurring between the two sectors with the addition of free schools and academies. These are both classed as state-funded, independent schools providing education at no charge to the parents or carers. This is explained in the next section.

Different types of state school

There is now a range of different governance structures in state schools from local authority or community schools to voluntary aided schools to foundation schools to trust schools to academies to the most recent free schools. This section highlights the main differences in the different types of school.

Local authority or community schools

These are schools where the employer is the local authority (LA) and staffing decisions are delegated to the governing body. There will be LA and community governors on the governing body. These schools all follow the same terms and conditions, known as the *Burgundy Book*: its full title is *The Conditions of Service for School Teachers in England and Wales*. They will have the same policies as other schools in the LA area and the same holidays.

Voluntary Aided and Voluntary Controlled schools

These types of school tend to have a religious character or faith and are very common among primary schools. In voluntary aided (VA) schools the actual employer of the staff is the governing body. On the governing body will be faith governors and they will be in the majority. The *Burgundy Book* explains that the standard conditions of service will have generally been incorporated into individual contracts of employment. VA schools can have different holiday dates from other schools in the county. VA schools also have an additional inspection but this is often conducted soon after an Ofsted inspection.

Voluntary controlled (VC) schools are similar to VA schools but the religious organization does not have the majority on the governing body and hence they are run by the LA. The terms and conditions for staff are then the same as community schools.

Foundation schools

These are very similar to VA schools in the eyes of employment law but without a religious dimension.

Academies

An academy is classed as an independent school but is funded by the government on the basis that no charge is made to pupils for their admission or education. The governing body is the employer of the teaching staff. As it is effectively an independent school it is up to the governing body to decide how far it wishes to incorporate the *Burgundy Book* into their standard contracts of employment. If the *Burgundy Book* is not used by an academy it must ensure that it publishes its own conditions of service. Academies can set their own holidays and sometimes have more radical school days or holiday calendars. For instance some academies have their INSET days on Saturdays. They also have no requirement to follow the National Curriculum.

Different types of school have become academies. Under the Labour government, it was often those that had poor exam results that became academies. This was not always the case as some very successful schools also became academies and took over less successful schools at the same time, forming a group of schools with an Executive Head and one governing body.

The Coalition government is encouraging schools to turn into academies with the greater freedom they have in terms of determining their curriculum. Schools which are judged as Outstanding can take a fast track route to academy status.

Trust schools

In autumn 2006 the previous government announced its intention to establish a new breed of school, the trust school. This was pitched to be somewhere between VA schools and academies. Trust schools can set their own terms and conditions but are likely to follow those of the LA. The trust holds the land and assets of the school in trust. The trust is the employer and sits apart from the governing body but on the governing body there will be trust governors. The full government definition of a trust school is a 'maintained foundation school supported by a charitable trust'.

Free schools

These are a new initiative of the Coalition government. Free schools are all-ability state-funded schools set up in response to parental demand. They can be established by charities, universities, businesses, educational groups, teachers and groups of parents.

Free schools will have same legal requirements as academies with their freedoms and flexibilities. Free schools have the ability to set their own pay and conditions for staff and a greater control of their budget. They have freedom from LA control, no requirement to follow the National Curriculum and the ability to change the length of terms and school days. Like academies, they will be funded on a comparable basis to other state-funded schools and will not be profit making.

Grammar schools

The term 'Grammar school' can mean different things across the country. Originally grammar schools were schools that selected children according to their ability through an exam, the 11+, taken in last year of primary school. In the 1970s many areas of the country replaced grammar schools with comprehensive schools. Some grammar schools became independent schools at this point other became comprehensive but retained the grammar school name.

There are some parts of the country that still have a grammar school system, such as Lincolnshire and Kent, as well as parts of other counties including Devon, the Wirral, Buckinghamshire and North Yorkshire. This also has an effect on the other secondary schools which were formerly known as secondary moderns. They are now called comprehensive schools but the reality is that the most able 35 per cent of pupils will be attending the grammar schools.

Overseas schools

A number of teachers choose at some stage in their career to work abroad. They may either work in an international school teaching children to speak English, often known as Teaching English as a Foreign Language (TEFL), or there are also overseas schools which offer a British curriculum. These are basically independent schools and are often members of the Independent Schools Council, the umbrella organization for independent schools.

Finally there are also overseas schools for the children of British Armed Forces members. This is known as Service Children's Education. There are primary schools in **Belgium, Germany, The Netherlands, Cyprus, Gibraltar, Falkland Islands, Belize and Brunei.** Secondary school provision is available for all pupils in North West Europe and Cyprus, whether at local secondary schools on a daily basis – or in boarding schools in Germany at Rheindahlen, Rinteln and Gütersloh. These are in effect state maintained but are overseas.

You need to be very careful that you are fully aware of the terms and conditions of employment in overseas schools. It can also be difficult to return to Britain to teach, as much due to the logistics of attending an interview as anything else. The result is that some teachers who work abroad have to have time without employment residing in Britain while they look for a job.

Other types of state and private school

There are even more types of school than have been previously mentioned. For example, there are Montessori schools which promote a certain style of teaching based on the works of the Italian physician and educator Maria Montessori. These are found in both the state and independent schools. There are also international schools which promote a certain country's education system. The overseas schools already mentioned are British International schools. In the UK there are international schools based on the education systems of other countries. These tend to also be independent schools.

Moving between schools

It is not that common for teachers to move between primary and secondary schools, as the curriculum is so different. In primary schools teachers have to teach the whole curriculum but in secondary schools teachers are subject specialists. You have to convince the school that you have the ability and skills to do this. If interviewers have candidates who fit the profile more closely they are less likely to take a risk on interviewing someone who is not currently doing that job.

In the independent sector it is more common for teachers to move between preparatory and secondary schools often because preparatory schools are more subject-specific than the state primary sector. In addition, at senior leadership level, teachers will move between preparatory schools and independent schools as they search for Headships and Deputy Headships.

Moving between the state and independent sectors is often dependent on the views of the interviewers. In the state sector some staff consider that teachers from the independent sector will not be able to cope with the larger classes and more challenging children. Some Heads of independent schools may reverse these prejudices and claim that state school teachers will not be able to fit in with the independent school community and will not be able to challenge the pupils appropriately.

Teachers who have worked in both sectors will recognize such views as archaic but the reality is that if you are looking for promotion or there are lots of candidates for the posts, interviewers have a tendency to play safe.

There are similar prejudices for people moving between grammar and comprehensive schools as interviewers may feel that teachers either will not be able to stretch the bright children enough or will not have the skills to deal with less able pupils. However, it is much easier for teachers to move between grammar and independent schools.

Final thoughts

There is no doubt that the current school you work in or the first school that you work in will limit your opportunities in the future. Some business recruitment experts suggest that professionals should also stay 'mainstream' to give themselves the most opportunities for career progression as the earlier you move into a more specialist sector the more you are pigeonholed there.

The situation is that there are fewer grammar, independent or middle schools than comprehensive secondary schools or state primary schools. So if you want more opportunities in the future and a greater flexibility for geographical placement then the latter schools are the safer choice.

However, many teachers love to work in certain sectors of education, feel most at home there and are more able to work effectively there. If you know which sector that is for you, then you are much better working there than trying to force yourself into a school outside your comfort zone.

Key points

1   The main types of school are maintained and independent or primary and secondary.
2   There are schools that straddle these polarities.
3   Different types of school will have different terms and conditions and it is important that you are aware of these.
4   Once you have worked in one sector of education it may not be easy to move to another.
5   Some recruiters argue the case of staying 'mainstream' to give greater opportunities for the future.
6   Some educationalists suggest you work in the type of school that suits your talents and personality best.

2 | Where to look for jobs

The basics

There are a huge number of places where teaching jobs are advertised and searching through all these could almost become a full time occupation in itself. However, not only do you do have to find job advertisements but you also need the time to think carefully about each application so that it is both strong and specific to that post.

Jobs in certain types of school will be advertised in different publications. Therefore an important part of finding a job vacancy is to establish the type of school you wish to work in. Chapter 1 (pages 13 to 22) has covered the legal differences and you should by now have an idea of the type of school you wish to work in. Or it may be that you do not have strong opinions about the type of school but prefer it to be within a specific geographical radius.

Even if you have a preference for the type of school in which you wish to work, you will still have to think carefully about geographical location. The majority of teachers normally have some idea of the areas that they can consider. The more specific the type of school the bigger effect this will have on the area you are searching. For example, if you have decided you wish to work in a state grammar school you will be restricted as there are not many areas of the country that have such a system. Part of your job search will then be to highlight those counties which operate such a system.

If you wish to work in an independent preparatory school you may have to look at your preferred general region rather than a specific county as even though there are preparatory schools all over the country, they are not concentrated in one county. On the other hand, if you have decided you wish to work in a state primary school, to make your search manageable you really need to highlight a county or set distance radius from a certain town or you will have too many jobs to be able to make strong applications for all of them.

This chapter aims to collect together the many publications where teaching jobs are advertised and suggest which is the most appropriate for certain types of school. All of these weblinks can be found on the companion website, so you can click straight through to them.

Identifying your starting point
◆ Where do you currently look for teaching posts?
◆ Do you prefer to use the internet or journals?
◆ Are there many jobs in the sector you are looking in?

The detail

There is a huge range of sources for vacancies and this has rapidly grown with the use of the internet. This chapter looks at the various sources and suggests the main sectors which are likely to place adverts at these locations.

Newspapers
The Times Educational Supplement   www.tes.co.uk
Arguably the largest source of teaching jobs is still *The Times Educational Supplement (TES)*. This covers all sectors of the profession. The adverts are also placed on their website which has a number of filtering features to enable you to locate the jobs of most interest. You can set up email alerts to notify you of jobs according to certain criteria. The newspaper is printed on a Friday and the website is continually updated.

Advertisements within *TES* can be expensive so there will be fewer part-time jobs in its pages. It is not the best location for main scale primary teaching posts as schools who feel they will receive lots of applicants may save money and look at other cheaper publications.

The Local Press   www.newspapersoc.org.uk
Probably the second largest source of adverts for jobs in schools is the local newspaper network. Local newspapers are a particularly good source of part-time and temporary jobs. If you did not live in the area you were looking to locate to, it used to be difficult to find such jobs but local newspapers now have websites with the jobs posted. The newspaper society has links to most local newspapers in the country and hence you can identify the newspapers which serve the area that you are interested in.

The Guardian   jobs.guardian.co.uk/jobs/education
Traditionally the national publication which has had the second highest number of teaching jobs has been the *Guardian* with its education section on a Tuesday. The *Guardian* has also been a good source for Higher Education jobs. You can also set up an email alert which sends you the jobs the day they are posted. The website appears to have a large number of jobs which are posted by recruitment agencies.

The Daily Telegraph   jobs.telegraph.co.uk
The Independent   jobs.independent.co.uk
The *Daily Telegraph* and the *Independent* are less well known for teaching jobs but they both have websites with education sections. Each newspaper has a range of jobs which seem to be posted by agencies.

Sec Ed   www.sec-ed.co.uk
Sec Ed is a national weekly newspaper for secondary schools which is published during term time on a Thursday. You can subscribe to an emailed copy free of charge. Placing job advertisements is very reasonably priced as there is a one-off fee for the year, so some large secondary schools regularly place their jobs in *Sec Ed* rather than *TES*.

Catholic Teachers Gazette   www.e-ctg.com
If you particularly wish to teach in an independent or state catholic school, the *Catholic Teachers Gazette* is the place to look; they also have a searchable website. It would, though, probably be wise to search other locations too.

Local authorities
If you are looking for a job in the state sector, the website of the local authority which you wish to work in is often a good source especially for local authority schools. As it is free for schools to place their adverts on the list, this can be a good place to look for primary and secondary main scale posts. There are often a large number of part-time and temporary positions on the lists too. You could do an internet search for the local authorities where you wish to work, or the prospects website has links to every local authority website in the country: ww2.prospects.ac.uk/cms/ShowPage/Home_page/Education/Teacher_Recruitment/p!ebdee?state=211

Local authorities used to manage a pool of teachers which you could apply to and then if you were successful you would be allocated a school. This is quite rare now but some local authorities may hold open days in the spring term which may allow you to visit several schools in the area. This tends to be more a feature of urban authorities. Some local authorities also operate their own supply pool which you can apply to and local schools will access before they use commercial agencies. The prospects website enables you to search those local authorities which operate such systems.

Websites and agencies

In addition to newspapers or journals that also place advertisements on-line there are a number of websites which have teaching jobs on them. Some of these websites are run by recruitment agencies and others by organizations for the good of a certain sector of education. This is not an exhaustive list of such websites as new ones are continually being established.

The Schools Recruitment Service
www.schoolsrecruitment.education.gov.uk

The Schools Recruitment Service was established by the previous government with the aim of improving and streamlining the recruitment of teaching staff. Job applications can be completed and sent on-line and previous applications can be saved and referred to again. It is possible to receive new adverts via email or texts. You can also place your details on-line in a 'talent pool' so that schools could search for people with the right profile for their vacancy. Currently half of the local authorities in England have signed up for the service but it is not necessarily widely used by schools.

Eteach   www.eteach.com

Eteach was probably one of the first websites to reach a high level of usage and is well worth visiting. It is said to be the UK's leading on-line recruitment service and is recommended by many of the professional organizations and teaching unions. Similarly to the *TES* website there is a virtual staff room which allows you to discuss educational issues with other teachers. There is a wide range of adverts across all sectors of the profession. You can place your profile on the site which allows employers to search for people.

The Independent Schools Council
www.isc.co.uk/JobZone_JobSearch.htm

The ISC shares an on-line vacancies service with the Independent Association of Preparatory Schools (IAPS). This should be the largest source of jobs in the independent sector as the two bodies represent the vast majority of independent schools and the service is free for its schools. In some ways this could be seen as comparable with a local authority representing all the state schools in its area. It also has teaching jobs in British International schools.

Gabbitas Education www.gabbitas.co.uk/teachers
Gabbitas is a long-established recruitment agency which specializes in the independent education sector both in the UK and overseas. Teachers are encouraged to register and submit their CVs and the agency will contact you if they feel there is an appropriate vacancy for you. They also have current vacancies on their website which you can view.

The Association of Muslim Schools
www.ams-uk.org/services/vacancies
The Association of Muslim Schools (AMS) represents both state and independent schools which have an Islamic character and lists current vacancies in their member schools.

Other websites
There are an increasing number of websites which have been established in recent years, such as:

www.education-jobs.co.uk
www.jobsineducation.co.uk
www.ukjobsnet.com/education-teaching-jobs
www.educationjobs.com
www.findersteachers.com

These offer many of the services of the other main teaching websites such as the facility to set up a profile and for adverts to be sent straight to you. It will be interesting to see how these develop over time and if one of them manages to subsume some of the other websites. It is worthwhile looking to see if any of them have developed a good coverage in your particular area.

Other agencies
If you are looking for temporary or supply work it is well-worth registering with the supply agencies in your area. There are national agencies which cover the country and also those which operate in one particular area. Some of the national agencies include:

www.capitaresourcing.co.uk/education
www.justteachers.co.uk
www.teachingpersonnel.com/go/schools
www.connex-education.com
www.hays.co.uk

Final thoughts

There is a danger that with so many possible avenues for finding job advertisements, you can spend all your time searching different websites and not actually applying for jobs. It is worthwhile making use of the email alerts on the different websites to send you your ideal jobs. It is important not to rely on this service though. Instead, highlight the one or two websites which seem to focus on the jobs you are particularly interested in and check those on a weekly basis.

Key points

1   Research the websites and identify those which focus on the jobs you are interested in.
2   Identify the local authorities which are within your travelling zone.
3   Set up email alerts with different websites.
4   Check the main websites for your jobs on a weekly basis.

How to structure your written application

The basics

The first impression that a school will get of you will be from your written application. It is very unlikely that you will ever get a job purely from a paper application. If you did you would have to wonder why! However, it is your written application that will get you to the first stage of the job process: an interview at the school. Many interviewers will pick out a front runner or two from the shortlisted group as a result of a strong written application. It may not be right but it is human nature that interviewers will be willing on such candidates to perform well and in some circumstances will be looking for the things you do well rather than focusing on less impressive parts of your performance.

One aspect of the recruitment process that I am constantly surprised by is the poor standard of so many written applications, some of which I can barely bring myself to read; as a result the candidate's time in sending the application has been wasted. There are some golden rules for completing written applications that will ensure your application does not fall onto this pile. Once you have made sure that the application is read the next stage is to begin to sharpen your application so that you are in the shortlisted application group. It is important to remember that a well written application will increase your chances of being shortlisted for a job that you are suited to, not one which you do not have the experience or skills for.

This chapter gives generic advice on how you can complete a strong written application. The chapter begins by considering how you can prepare yourself to write your application before studying the three main elements of written applications; the curriculum vitae (CV), application form and the letter of application. This chapter presents advice which would be relevant for any post: in Section Two (pages 89 to 146) of this book more specific guidance will be offered on particular roles. Hence this chapter does not give specific examples of applications as these are included in Section Two. Once you have read this chapter you will have a better understanding of why the applications in Section Two have been constructed in the way they have.

Identifying your starting point

◆ Have you completed a written application before?
◆ What advice have colleagues or peers given on your application?
◆ Did your previous application(s) help you gain an interview?
◆ Have you any thoughts on the strengths or weakness of your application?

The detail

Preparation

To begin to structure your written application you will be in one of two positions. The first is that you have seen an advertisement for a job that you wish to apply for, the other that you have decided the type of post you wish to apply for and are currently constructing a practice application while you have some spare time. The key here is that you know the post you wish to gain.

You then need to consider why you are suited to this post? You may tackle this question by completing a brainstorm, making bullet points or writing your thoughts down in paragraph form. These notes are the cornerstone around which you will be constructing your application.

The second key part of preparation is understanding what type of school the job is advertised at or whether you have decided on a particular type of school that you wish to work in. From an interviewer's perspective it is apparent that many candidates have not really considered this aspect of their applications. So once you have identified the type of school you need to think carefully about why you wish to work in this type of school and, even better, why *this* school specifically? Again, record your thoughts as you will wish to draw upon these as you construct your application.

You then need to look at the details of the application procedure, such as the closing date for applications. Do you need to contact the school for further details or are those details already on a website? Is there an application form for the post or should you send a CV? How do you submit your application? Is there the opportunity to send your application electronically in addition to, or instead of, using the post?

The final part of the jigsaw in job application preparation is to consider objectively how good a match for the post you are. This topic will be considered in more detail in Chapter 4 (pages 43 to 52). It may be at this point you choose to move to Chapter 4 before returning to this chapter to complete your application.

If you want to see examples of this guidance put into practice, then Section Two (pages 89 to 146) of this book has a range of CVs and letters of application on which you can model your own.

Curriculum vitae (CV)

Increasingly schools are not necessarily asking for CVs. One of the major reasons for this is that in the state sector the application form will be part of the school's response to the safeguarding agenda and will enable a school to ensure that they have all the information about a candidate that they require. You must never send a CV instead of a completed application form. Some schools will immediately discard such applications.

CVs are often requested by independent schools, however, and they may also be requested in the state sector for senior leadership positions, as the standard local authority teacher application form may not allow a senior leader to give all the factual information they require. CVs are frequently requested by overseas schools at all levels and by recruitment agencies.

Finally, if you are trying to prepare yourself for a future job search, constructing a CV and keeping it current can be an excellent method of ensuring that you have all the factual information which you will ever require for an application form in one place. You can then simply copy and paste the information from your CV into the form. Maintaining a CV in this way can also be a good way of auditing your skills and considering if there are elements of your profile which you need to develop.

You should try to keep your CV to two sides of A4 paper. One way of achieving this is to carefully consider how you lay out your CV and ensure you use bullet points for many of your statements. The main text should not be less than font size 11. You might choose to use font size 12 for important statements such as the name of the school that you work in. Finally you might increase the size of text to 14 for titles such as 'Employment History' or 'Qualifications'. Never use more than one font in your CV – standard choices are

Arial, Calibri or Times New Roman. Rather than using a different font, for more individuality use italics or bold. However, even with these guidelines you need to be careful that your CV does not start to look messy.

There are two types of CV; a chronological CV and functional CV. A chronological CV is based around recording your employment history in date order whereas a functional CV emphasizes your skills and expertise.

Chronological CVs

A chronological CV is a very factual document, the major part of which is your employment history. Typically a chronological CV will begin with your personal details, then employment history, education and interests before finishing with your references.

If you are making steady progress in your school and have obviously made good choices in your career structure this type of CV will demonstrate your career progression. Perhaps you are looking at an Assistant Headship position in a secondary school and have moved from teacher, to Head of Department to Head of Faculty to a whole school project. This type of CV will immediately highlight this information in an easily understandable way for a recruiter. If you do not have many major key achievements but have focused on performing your job description very competently a chronological CV is a strong choice.

If you have gaps in your employment history or have tackled a variety of jobs such a CV will make these points very obvious. If you are looking for a change of direction in your career or to gain a significant promotion such a CV will not enable you to really sell yourself and you will be relying on your letter of application to do this for you. If you are at the start of your teaching career but have made some key achievements before becoming a teacher, a chronological CV will not be best suited to you.

Figure 3.1 gives an example of how you can structure your employment history and the extra detail that you may include in this section for a chronological CV. Template 1 provides the full structure and headings for a chronological CV.

Figure 3.1: Employment history

Employment

2006 –Present: Brockdale High (11–19 co-ed comprehensive, 1150 NOR)
Lead teacher of English – Led a faculty of eight full time equivalent teachers. Implemented a new scheme of work for English GCSE, raising the GCSE pass rate from 65 per cent to 77 per cent over four years.

2002–2006 Beacon School (11–16 co-ed comprehensive, 850 NOR)
Head of Year – Oversaw the pastoral development of a year group from year 8 until they left the school. Implemented an academic mentoring system which saw the lowest exclusion rate for a year 11 group in my time at the school.

2000–2002 Beacon School
Teacher of English …

Functional CVs
Whereas a chronological CV begins with your employment history, a functional CV begins with your key achievements and you only give a brief note about each post you have held in the employment history.

Functional CVs are ideal if you have followed a less traditional career structure or if you are eager for promotion. Perhaps your previous positions have been as a main scale teacher but you are looking to become a Head of Faculty. A chronological CV will make it obvious that you have not held a leadership position. However, if you have led different projects as a classroom teacher, delivered INSET sessions or conducted some academic research you can use the key achievements section to immediately bring this to the attention of a recruiter.

If you have moved around a variety of different posts or have left the profession at different times, a functional CV can be ideal as you can use it to highlight *what you have achieved* in those posts rather than emphasizing the *range* of different posts you have held.

If you have lots of achievements and you struggle to fit them all into your letter of application, a functional CV can be ideal to ensure that the recruiter can see them. If you are a more mature candidate and looking to make a significant promotion for the first time a functional CV takes the spotlight away from how long you have been in one post or in one school and instead highlights what you have achieved as a teacher.

If you are moving from one sector to another, such as private to state, or moving from a secondary school to a preparatory school, a functional CV will enable you to focus on your transferable skills and experiences.

Figure 3.2 gives an example of a key achievements section of functional CV. Template 2 provides the full structure and headings for a functional CV.

Figure 3.2: Key achievements

Key achievements
- ◆ Led the accreditation for the Healthy Schools Award.
- ◆ Implemented a PSHE programme for Key Stage 2.
- ◆ Deliver weekly assemblies to Key Stage 2 pupils addressing the PLTS agenda.
- ◆ Level 1 hockey coach.

Personal profiles
If you look at CVs prepared by employment agencies there is often a personal profile. This is two or three sentences which describe you and the type of role you are looking for. It is a fascinating process to try to summarize your experiences and aspirations in such a short number of words and one that is worth practising in preparation for interview as well as for a CV. Some employers suggest that a personal profile can be off-putting and they should only be used by employment agencies. In some ways it probably depends on the type of sector you are applying to, for example if you are applying for a very traditional institution perhaps a personal profile should be omitted

Figure 3.3 gives an example of a personal profile from a functional CV. This is written in the first person and summarizes key elements of the candidate's job application.

Figure 3.3: Personal profile

> **Personal profile**
>
> I am an effective middle leader with strong experience of developing an already high achieving Science Faculty. My leadership draws upon my outstanding classroom teaching (Ofsted 2009) and further professional studies for the Chartered Institute of Educational Assessors.

Golden rules for CVs
- Think carefully as to whether a functional or chronological CV is right for you.
- Never send a CV instead of an application form if asked for. A form is often used for safeguarding purposes to collect very specific and consistent information.
- Only use one font in a CV.
- Be consistent in your font size: one size for titles, another for key points and slightly smaller for longer points.

Application forms
Application forms are generally one of the most straightforward elements to job hunting but it's surprising how many candidates do this section badly. Most schools will now have an electronic version of their application form, in which case you should complete it electronically too. Schools expect a level of ICT competence whether it is for using an interactive whiteboard during a lesson, completing an electronic register or writing pupil reports on-line. If you have completed an application form on-line you are immediately showing a school that you have these skills. It also means that the days of worrying about the neatness of your handwriting or making errors on a form are now gone.

Much of an application form is factual information and you need to make sure that it is correct. I see many application forms where candidates have obviously made errors on the dates of their qualification or I am left confused as to how long they have been in certain posts as the dates do not marry up. If you have gathered this information on your CV, you should then be able to copy and paste this into the form.

You also need to double check that you have completed all the boxes, paying particular attention to items like your teacher reference number (which some of you may recognize as your DfE, DfEE or even DES number) or the criminal convictions question. Many candidates for some reason accidentally forget to complete these and then the employer is left worrying if the candidate has something to hide!

Where you can begin to make your application form stronger is in two sections: the employment history section and the further details section. In the employment history, there may be room to add bullet points of what you have achieved in each role. You need to remember that an application form is more for facts and the letter of application is to highlight these facts and suggest why they are relevant to your application for the role.

Many candidates are confused as to the section for further details and how this compares with the letter of application. Some candidates will choose to do one or the other and not both. This is always a mistake. One of the problems many candidates have is getting their message across in the limited space available and the section on the form for further information is a real aid in tackling this difficulty. The application forms that I prefer reading are those that use the further details section to explain what the candidate does in their particular post. This can be communicated in bullet points rather than continuous prose if preferred. You can then use your letter of application to relate the most important of these to the role that you are applying for with some justification. Using this system ensures that your letter will always be less than two sides of A4.

Golden rules for application forms
◆ Always try to word process your application form.
◆ Ensure there is something in every box.
◆ Double check that the dates in your employment history and education are correct.
◆ Ensure the further information dovetails with your letter of application.
◆ Include information from your letter and other additional information.
◆ Be prepared to have to explain any gaps in service.

Letters of application
There is an increasing habit for candidates not to write a formal letter of application but instead to send a brief email with their attached application form. Your letter of application is the key selling point in your armoury and I would always encourage you to spend time on writing this properly.

The best letters of applications show a coherent structure and, in the words of one of my former Principals should tell a story. Most strong candidates use the same structure for the opening and ending paragraphs of their letter. There is a greater variation in the middle paragraphs of the letter. Templates 3, 4 and 5 give suggestions for classroom teachers, middle leaders and senior leaders of how you may wish to organize your letter; the section below offers some suggestions for appropriate paragraphs.

The first paragraph of your letter should be short, covering no more than the job you are applying for and where you have seen it is advertised. If you are very short of space in the rest of your letter some candidates will instead use a reference e.g. Ref: Teacher of English Advertised in the *Chorley Guardian* on 7th January.

Figure 3.4: Opening paragraph

> I am very excited to apply for the post of Teacher of Biology at Highfields School advertised in *The Times Educational Supplement* on 9th May.

The second paragraph should briefly explain why you are applying for the job. It is likely that this will be related to your current post and your main skills and attributes. One thing that many candidates miss at this point is to comment on why they wish to work at this particular school and as a result the reader may be concerned that the candidate is submitting the same letter for a multitude of jobs. If you can highlight the school at this point you will be making a connection with the reader who will hence be more open to the rest of your letter.

The second paragraph of a candidate applying for a year 4 class teacher position may look like Figure 3.5.

Figure 3.5: Extract from a year 4 class teacher application

> I have been teaching the year 2 class at Palm Primary for the last three years. I have developed a strong range of teaching skills in this time and have a particular interest in developing literacy in boys. The Hawthorns has an excellent reputation among local educationalists as a child-centred school and I have studied your recent Ofsted report with interest. One of the issues that Ofsted commented upon was the literacy initiative that you have developed across the curriculum. I would relish the opportunity to be involved in such an initiative.

There are perhaps two broad methods for tackling the middle section of the letter. The first is to use a chronological structure of what you have achieved in your current post. The second is to consider the headings within the job profile and ensure that each paragraph tackles these headings. One of the common errors that strong candidates make at this point is that their writing concentrates on what they have done. To hone your letter even further what you should be aiming to do is not only write about what you have done but to also say what you learnt from this and how these experiences will mean that you can hit the ground running when the school offers you the job.

You need to carefully consider any acronyms or project titles that you use. For example if you're applying for a job in the independent sector but are currently in the state sector the reader may not have a full grasp of what APP (Assessing Pupils' Progress) is or specialist school status, so try to explain such terms. In addition, some of the groupings at your school may be particular to this location. For example, the Senior Leadership Team could be called the Central Management Team, Senior Team or School Management Team in other schools.

Figure 3.6: An extract from a preparatory school Art teacher applicant

I firmly believe I should seek to inspire those pupils who struggle with Art and Design in year 7 and 8 as well the more able students. I often find that in Key Stage 2 pupils are eager to display their work but as we begin to prepare for Common Entrance pupils become more conscious of how skilled their designs are. I believe that with a good grasp of perspective any child can begin to understand how to develop their drawing. I used the school photography competition as an inspiration with the aim of taking a photograph which best demonstrated perspective. The children took some fantastic photographs and we then used photocopies to identify different elements of perspective. At the end of the year all the year 7 and year 8 pupils wished to display their work in our annual art show and one pupil came second in the national competition. Interestingly, this is a child who did not want to display their work in year 7. I am eager to develop these skills further in your school by integrating your rich ICT facilities into the teaching of Art.

Within the middle section of your letter it is worth including a paragraph about your vision of education related to the particular role. So if you are applying for a main scale post you need to give an idea of what you are looking to achieve in your classroom. As Head of Department you will present your thoughts as to the role of your subject within the school and as a senior leader you will be describing a much wider vision of education.

The paragraph on the previous page (Figure 3.6) is by a preparatory school Art teacher who describes his vision for Art through a successful project he has delivered and links this to facilities at the school he is applying to.

For main scale teachers I like to see a paragraph about an actual lesson that has been particularly successful with an explanation of why this was the case. This begins to give a strong indication that you are a good teacher. If you can include evidence from an Ofsted observation or an internal school evaluation of the grade of the lesson, even better! The following paragraph could be written by an applicant for French position.

Figure 3.7: An extract from an ITT MFL (Initial Teacher Training Modern Foreign Languages) applicant

I have greatly enjoyed the opportunity to teach French by implementing the I Languages scheme. I strongly believe modern foreign languages provide a wonderful opportunity to teach students about different cultures in addition to communication. In a recent lesson looking at daily routine, my year 7 pupils looked at the routines of four children in France, Quebec, The Ivory Coast and Haiti. In addition to developing their knowledge of reflexive verbs we also discussed the well being of those children. My pupils finished the lesson by writing a postcard to pupils in our partner school in Haiti. This lesson was observed by my ITT co-ordinator at the school and graded as Outstanding.

Many teachers will also include a paragraph about their view on pastoral issues. For a main scale teacher this may consider their potential role as form tutor. A middle leader may address how they support other staff with pupil issues. A senior leader on the other hand could consider their experiences of delivering whole school assemblies or managing complex incidents. The follow paragraph could be written by an applicant for a second-in-department post.

Figure 3.8: Extract from second-in-department applicant

> I currently act as a tutor to a year 10 class and have greatly enjoyed helping these pupils develop over the last three years. I particularly like being able to form effective relationships with students, thereby ensuring that they feel able to access any support they need to fulfil their potential. I am familiar with the legal and safeguarding requirements demanded of schools. I am sure that these experiences would enable me to help and support other colleagues in the department with any pupil issues that may develop and I would also prove an invaluable support to both my Head of Department and also my Head of Year.

The final paragraphs are then often much more standard. A good penultimate paragraph will consider your wider experience and how you could use this to move the school forward, for example if there is an extra-curricular activity that you will be prepared to offer. This is the one paragraph that does not need to be about the core job and in many ways is the icing on the cake for the reader. It is important to remember that any activity you present in your letter and then discuss at interview, a school could reasonably expect you to deliver. The following paragraph could be written by any applicant for a secondary school teaching post.

Figure 3.9: Example of an extra-curricular paragraph

> During my career I have always enjoyed taking part in the whole life of the school, particularly through extra-curricular activities such as running school tennis teams. In recent years I have, for example, led trips to Eastbourne for the pre-Wimbledon tournament as a reward for pupils who have umpired primary school tennis matches. In my current post I have also enjoyed helping the pupils run stalls during Fair Trade Fortnight to promote this important cause.

The last paragraph should succinctly highlight in no more than two or three sentences why you are the perfect candidate for the post. You should also include the niceties of thanking the reader for considering your application and hoping that you have the opportunity to meet the reader at interview. The following extract could be written by a senior leader applicant but there are also phrases which could be drawn on by any applicant.

Figure 3.10: Example of a senior leader's final paragraph

I have a core belief that every young person is entitled to experience a valuable, inclusive and individualized education in which they are engaged with their learning. As a senior leader this belief gives me the energy and passion to remain positive even when dealing with moments of crisis. I believe that I have the people skills, along with a passion for teaching and learning, that will ensure I am a vital member of your senior leadership team. I would like to thank you for considering my application and I hope that I will have the opportunity to meet you at interview.

You may be fortunate enough to have one item that is your unique selling point that few other candidates have. This may be the point that means you get interviewed even when there are more experienced teachers applying. You may have had an academic paper published, played sport at a high level or be very skilled in the arts. The important thing about such a talent is not to devote your whole letter to this point but instead when you do mention it, highlight the positives of this to the reader.

Finally, take care over the presentation of your letter. The advertisement may direct you to an administrator within the school for obtaining an application form and job details but it is worthwhile taking the time to find out the Headteacher's name and addressing your letter to that person or sending a quick email to the school asking whom the letter should be addressed to (if this is not stated on the application details).

Always use the business letter layout conventions. If you are short of space there is no reason why you should not shorten the school address to the person, post and the school's name. Now is not the time to use fancy fonts; instead be conservative and use something like Arial, Calibri or Times New Roman with a minimum point size of 12. Your letter must not exceed two pages, but you can change the margins on your letter to give you some space. Remember to use your CV or the further information section on the application form to include more of your experience rather than writing more than two pages. Finally, make sure the application arrives on time with the correct postage. A belt and braces approach is to both email and post your application pack. In an ideal world an emailed application should arrive at least a day before the closing date.

Golden rules for letters of application
- You must word process your letter.
- It is always a good idea to ask someone to proof read your letter.
- Always personalize your letter to the school that you are applying to.
- Always use a standard letter layout including the location of the address on the page.
- Use prose not bullet points.
- Check whom the letter should be addressed to.
- The minimum font size you should use is point 12.
- Keep your letter to less than two pages.

Final thoughts

Your written application is crucial to you getting an interview. There is no excuse for not ensuring this is done properly. It is a good idea to begin thinking and planning your application before posts appear by keeping a good record of your career and some notes on why this experience is useful. It can be worthwhile seeing if you can read other people's applications and also to look at the examples in this book but never copy another application. You may also find there are people who are prepared to help you improve your letter such as a trusted colleague or friend.

Key points

1   Spend time preparing for applications even before there is an appropriate job advertised.
2   A frequently updated CV can be a good method of keeping a record of what you have done and how this applies to the type of job you are looking for.
3   Choose whether a functional or chronological CV is most appropriate for you.
4   Ensure your application form is carefully completed and is a strong record of what you have done.
5   The letter of application is vital; this is the document that applies your experience to the post.

4 | How strong is your application?

The basics

One of the challenges you will face in your job search is assessing how strong the application that you have constructed actually is. It is likely that when you see a job being advertised you will wonder whether it is worth you spending the time applying. You may assess this by asking yourself two questions:

◆ Will the school consider my application?
◆ Will there be people better qualified than me?

If you then decide to submit an application but do not get an interview, you should ask yourself whether it was worthwhile you putting together your application.

In the previous chapter, we looked at how you could structure your application to make it stronger. After reading this chapter you will have a better idea of how you can analyse your personal suitability for a post or a school. It is important that you use this information and draw upon it in your application. You may feel that your application is strong for certain reasons but unless you explain this the interviewer may not recognize these strengths. You will also have a clearer idea of the process that an interviewer will go through in shortlisting for posts. Finally, we will consider where you can obtain further advice to strengthen your applications.

Identifying your starting point
◆ What post do you wish to apply for?
◆ What type of school do you wish to work in?
◆ How do these compare with your current situation?
◆ Have you received any offers of interviews?
◆ Have you asked for advice on your letter of application?

The detail

Comparison between roles

Recruiters often want to play safe. They will be looking for a candidate whose experience looks the best fit for the role they are advertising. What you are trying to show in your application is that you are not a risky proposition.

The closer your current role is to the post you are applying for, the stronger your application is likely to be. There are two factors that you could consider here:

1   How close is the specialism of the advertised role to your current position or the one you are being trained for?
2   How similar is your current post in hierarchical terms to the advertised post?

For **classroom teachers** this role specialism will vary according to the phase of education you are working in. In primary schools the specialism of the role is likely to relate to the year of the pupils and in a secondary school it will revolve around the subject being taught but may also take account of the level of qualification that you are currently delivering. For **primary student teachers** or **main scale teachers**, you will be a stronger candidate if the class you currently teach is a similar age to that of the advertised post. A school may also be looking for a teacher who is interested in the particular subject area that is currently missing from the school.

For **secondary school teachers** it is likely that the role you are applying for is the same as that you have trained for or currently work in. Look for other similarities too: is the examination syllabus the same, are the schemes of work similar or what about the type of interactive whiteboard or ICT system? There is no reason why you cannot apply for a job that is slightly outside your field especially if the role combines two subjects or if you feel that the school will not receive many applications.

For **leadership posts** there has been a tradition for them to be broadly divided into two groups, either pastoral or curriculum. At a middle leadership level this divide may be seen through Head of Year positions or curriculum leader roles. At senior leadership level the distinction is likely to be hazier. The role may not be labelled as one or the other and it may only be from studying the job description that you can decide if the role is directed more in one direction than another.

One of the difficulties in comparing roles beyond that of a classroom teacher is the size of a school. Being a Head of Year in a 500-pupil secondary school is very different from being a Head of Year in a 2000-pupil secondary school. There used to be a system of middle leadership responsibility points which started at 1 and went up to 5. This made it far easier to compare roles. This has now changed to Teaching and Learning Responsibilities where there is a TLR1 scale and a TLR2 scale. One of the difficulties with this system is that schools can set their own pay rates within these scales.

Table 4.1: Comparing hierarchies in different sized secondary schools

Small Secondary School (Up to 600 pupils)	Medium Secondary School (600–1000 pupils)	Large Secondary School (More than 1000 pupils)
Main Scale Teacher	Main Scale Teacher	Main Scale Teacher
Head of Department Year Leader	Second in Department	Subject Key Stage Coordinator Assistant Head of Year
Head of Faculty	Head of Department Year Leader	Second in Department
Head of Key Stage	Head of Faculty	Head of Department
Assistant Head	Head of Key Stage	Head of Faculty
Assistant Head	Assistant Head	Head of Key Stage is an Assistant Head

This table attempts to give an idea of the relative seniority of posts in different schools. The closer your current position is in the hierarchy to the post you are applying for, the stronger your application is likely to be. Some recruiters have used a rule of thumb to state that if the post is more than two rungs above your current position then your application will not be very strong. For example, in certain subject areas you may be able to go from main scale teacher to a Head of Faculty post in a small school. However, if you are applying for a role in a large secondary school where there may be 15 teachers in a faculty, it is unlikely that as a main scale teacher you would be able to construct a strong enough application for a Head of Faculty post.

Where this type of analysis can fall down is when you are a teacher in a small school and you have volunteered for lots of tasks. It may then be you have a much broader experience than a colleague in a larger school where those tasks have been allocated to people in hierarchical positions.

It is much harder to construct such a table for primary school, middle leader and classroom teacher positions. In fact the reverse situation many even be found in primary schools. In those small primary schools which consist of only three classes, many Heads will consider that it needs a more experienced teacher to cope with the demands of teaching a class which contains pupils from three different National Curriculum years.

At a senior leadership level it is much easier to compare posts as there is a national leadership spine and you can easily see if the Assistant Headship post in a large school is equivalent to the sole deputy position in a much smaller school. You can then use this knowledge to determine how similar your current post is to the one that you are aiming for.

Comparing schools
One of the hardest things for you to reconcile as a job hunter is the attitude of some educationalists towards different types of school and how they perceive you will fit into theirs. This has already been covered in Chapter 1 (pages 13 to 22) with the discussion of moving between different schools.

If you are trying to assess how strong your application is for another school, you need to see what comparisons you can make between your current and potential placements. It is much more obvious if you are looking at schools in the same sector. So if you are working in a state grammar school and applying for another state grammar this similarity will make your application stronger.

Other factors you could consider are the attainment results of the pupils. These could be similar for an independent school and a state school and if you can point out this similarity your application will be stronger. If there are corresponding socio-economic backgrounds of the pupils of your current school and the one you are applying for, highlighting this can make your application stronger. We have considered the size of the school in terms of pupil numbers but another similarity could be the number of staff. An independent school with far fewer pupils than a state school may have a similar number of staff due to their small class sizes. If you are applying for a leadership post the experience of dealing with similar numbers of staff is worth highlighting.

Person specifications

One of the most straightforward methods of assessing your suitability for a post is if the school distributes a person specification. This will link the skills for the role into two sections: those which are essential and those which are desirable.

If a school has taken the time to collect the skills together into this type of table, they are being serious that they expect the candidate to have all the essential attributes. There may be occasions when you can be lucky and get to an interview without one of the essential attributes but on the whole you need to have all of them.

You may say that the school may not receive many applications and then it is worth the gamble of applying for the post. This may be the case but in such circumstances it is not uncommon for the school to either re-advertise or seek a different solution to the job vacancy by changing its specification. The desirable section can be considered as more of the school's wish list and you should not necessarily worry if you are lacking some of these elements as such factors can be equalized by a very well written application which sells your strengths.

You must ensure that you make it clear to the interviewer that you have the skills they are looking for. You may struggle to put all the evidence in your letter of application and this is where either a personalized functional CV or making full use of the further information section of the application form can be vital.

Getting the basics right

Your application will obviously be stronger if you can get the basics right and in many ways there is no excuse for not achieving this. One reason that job hunters give for not getting the basics right is that they do not have enough time! If you feel you do not have enough time because you are applying for too many posts, and this can be a particular issue for student teachers, then perhaps you should focus on the jobs you would really like. If you send one less application a week but those that you send are of a higher quality this may be far more effective. If you do not feel you have enough time because your current post is so all consuming, you need to seriously think how much do you want this new job? If you do really want the job then you must give the application the same focus that you give to your current job.

If you are just not a detail person then you need to ask someone to check through your application. They do not have to be in the education profession but somebody who will check that things like the dates are correct and all the boxes are completed on the application form. Also to check that information in the letter is correct. You would not believe how many candidates make an error on the school's name in a letter as they are copying and pasting a previous application.

It would be a good idea to refer back to Chapter 3 and check that you have followed the golden rules (page 42). Lastly, never submit an application in haste. It is so easy to complete a form or letter electronically and then immediately email it. It is good practice to always send that email the next day when you have read your application through one more time.

How will your application be judged?

Unfortunately, however much time and energy you spend on your application, interviewers are unlikely to spend the same amount of time reading it. If a school has more than 20 applications for the post, the first read through may be very cursory with the interviewer reading little more than each application for the post and deciding if the candidates are strong, average or unsuitable. At this preliminary stage applications may be put on one of the lower priority piles not through a lack of skills but due to not getting the basics right such as the application being late, a poor standard of written English or the application procedure not being followed, e.g. no letter of application.

The next stage in assessing applications may be a grading system. One Headteacher I have worked for graded all applications on a scale of A, B or C. A meant definitely interview, B meant maybe interview and C meant he would not interview the candidate. He would then introduce a more detailed scaling with the addition of pluses and minuses by making notes on the candidates' strengths such as the quality of their education, their passion for the post, their wider skills and relevance of their experience.

Some interviewers will tackle the whole process far more scientifically and compare each letter of application with the job profile and score the candidates. Candidates will only be interviewed if they can demonstrate every essential quality and then the desirable qualities will effectively act as the 'tiebreaker' to decide who is interviewed. This system tends to be used more when schools recognize that they may have to justify their process. This can happen in the event of a restructuring of the school or a local re-organization of education. It may also be used if there are internal candidates or known external candidates applying. Schools may be more likely to use such a process if they are advertising for lots of posts and the Headteacher wishes to delegate the shortlisting process. Finally, the more senior the role being advertised the more likely a scoring system will be used.

Whom can you seek advice from?

The previous section shows that not all schools will be rigorously scientific in the manner that they shortlist candidates for interview. This can be frustrating when you have given so much care to an application. If you are not being successful with your applications it is worthwhile seeking some guidance and feedback.

The first place to ask is your own school. If you are a student teacher on placement, you could ask the senior leader who is the link to the Higher Education establishment. It is likely that this person will be able to give you better advice than your mentor who may not actually shortlist many written applications.

If you are currently working in a school it can feel awkward to ask for advice from a line manager. It can be easier if you are looking for promotion. An alternative is if there is senior leader from the school who has recently retired or joined another school. It is often worthwhile informally asking the opinions of your colleagues either at your current school or at different schools to see if they can help.

There may also be local authority advisors who could help you. The website twitter is currently proving popular with teachers sharing information and if you have established a reasonable number of followers, one of them may be prepared to help you.

If a job is advertised by a recruitment agency, they will often be prepared to give you feedback on the quality of your written applications. You may see that an agency is advertising jobs of a certain type that you are interested in and you could approach them in advance to look at your application.

Your union or professional organization may hold workshops on application techniques. If you attend one of these you will probably find that at the end of the session they will run a clinic providing one-to-one advice on written applications.

One thing that you need to be careful of is not to seek advice from too many people at the same time as they may offer conflicting advice which can then confuse. Often the best course of action is to seek advice from one person and re-work your application accordingly. If you are still not successful in being shortlisted then ask for advice from other people.

Many people wonder if they should ask the school they have applied to for feedback on the written application. I would suggest it is doubtful that you will receive helpful advice as many schools will probably fob off you with some anodyne comments. The time when they may give you some useful feedback is if you personally know the recruiter at the school but be aware that such feedback may be upsetting.

Final thoughts

There is no doubt that the more ambitious you are in your job search the weaker your application will be in comparison with more experienced candidates and the harder it will be to reach interview. Examples of this can be if you are trying to move to a very different type of school and be promoted at the same time or if the promotion you are seeking is a considerable step up.

Your application will be strengthened if you can highlight the similarities between your current school and role to the one that you are applying for. It is vital that you ensure that you cover the basics of job application and do not make silly mistakes in the pursuit of applying for too many jobs.

Person specifications can be helpful in identifying whether you are a strong candidate for the post at the outset and can be vital in putting together a good application by showing you have the requisite skills and abilities for the posts. You also need to be aware that no matter how strong your application, not all schools will rigorously assess your suitability for the post as you would hope.

If you are not being shortlisted and offered interviews for the posts it is worthwhile considering who can give you advice on your application though it can be unhelpful to receive views from lots of different people.

Key points

1   Ask yourself how similar your school and role are to the post you are applying for.
2   Use your application to highlight these similarities.

3   You should carefully map yourself against the person specification and use this to frame your application.
4   If you are not being offered interviews seek individual advice on your application

What interview tasks could you face?

The basics

Hopefully after following the advice in the previous chapters on structuring your application you will now be the proud recipient of a letter, email or phone call inviting you for interview. In many schools the term 'interview' is quite misleading as the interview will be only one element of the process which decides whether you will be offered the job.

The selection process you participate in may be brief or lengthy. For a main scale post with few applicants it could last just a morning or an afternoon. In the case of some senior leadership posts, the selection process could occur over three consecutive days.

The duration of the process will, of course, depend on the number of tasks that is included. It is important that you realize that there will be formal selection tasks and also those that are informal. Many applicants purely focus on tasks which are labelled as such on the interview schedule and forget all the informal moments during the day/s which are also likely to form part of the process.

In this chapter we will consider a variety of formal selection tasks such as teaching a lesson, giving a presentation, completing an in-tray exercise and the various panel interviews you may face. The final formal interview will be considered in more detail in the next chapter.

So what are informal selection tasks? Basically you are on interview for the whole time you are at the school so from the moment your car enters the school grounds, and even before, people will be making judgements about you and in many cases their views will be gathered. In this chapter advice will be given on how you can make the most of that part of the selection process too.

Identifying your starting point
◆ What interview tasks have you participated in previously?

- What feedback did you get on your performance from the interviewer?
- How will this feedback affect your 'behaviour' at your next interview?
- What tasks are included in the selection day you are attending?
- Which of these do you feel are your strengths and why?
- Which of the tasks would you like further advice on?

The detail

You will probably find that as the seniority of the post increases so does the number of tasks. It is rare now for a classroom teacher to not have to teach a lesson and this may be the only other formal task in addition to the final interview. A curriculum middle leader may have to deliver a presentation while a pastoral middle leader may be asked to complete an in-tray exercise. At Assistant Headship and Deputy Headship level you may be asked to complete all these tasks listed above in addition to some smaller interviews.

For the post of Headteacher, the tasks on selection days can vary greatly from school to school and much of this is down to the fact that this is the one position in a school where the governors, usually non-educationalists, run the process and decide on the tasks. They may have their own views on certain tasks drawn from their life experiences.

Delivering a lesson

Of all the tasks that you will face during your interview, as a classroom teacher and middle leader, this is the one that you must get right. You may fluff your formal interview and stumble over every answer but if a senior leader observes you deliver an 'Outstanding' lesson you will still have an excellent chance of being offered the role.

One of the keys to this task is careful preparation. This is one of the few times in your career when you only have to deliver one lesson in a school day so it is vital that you have it carefully planned. Your starting point is to be clear about what you have been asked to deliver and what the nature of the group is.

If you feel the lesson objective is ambiguous, there is nothing wrong with you clarifying the task with the school, often an email is the easiest way of doing this as it may be difficult to speak directly with the middle leader who has decided the title. However, do not forget that sometimes interview lessons are purposefully ambiguous to give candidates a greater licence to show their creativity.

Try to gather as much information on the pupils as you can. Ask for details on how many pupils will be in the group, what level they are currently working at and what progress the school is hoping the pupils will make by the end of the Key Stage. Then compare this with the academic profile of the school available via published data. If this is a high performing school, the pupils will be expected to be stretched and to make rapid progress in the lesson. With schools whose performance is lower you will have to use your judgement from the data that the school has given you as to how much progress they should be making in the lesson.

If the school informs you that there are interactive whiteboards available you must make some effort to incorporate this into your teaching. You may be wary of using the interactive features of the whiteboard especially if the software is different from that you are used to so instead the minimum would be to use the whiteboard simply as a projector to display images important to your lesson.

You would be ill advised to change your style of teaching for a single lesson; instead, stay within your normal character and ensure this lesson is tightly focused. Have a very clear lesson plan which the observer or observers can follow. It is not uncommon for observers to swap over during the lesson and if there is a clear lesson plan they can then pick up on what has already been covered. You must have a definite structure to your lesson and most observers would expect to see the minimum of a three-part lesson with a clear starter and main body of a lesson and then a plenary where you can clearly assess the progress the pupils have made. If the lesson does not move as quickly as you would have hoped it is tempting to omit the plenary. Rather than doing this it is often a good idea to include a supplementary task which you may use if there is time or leave out if necessary.

If you have time why not practise your lesson in your own school before the interview? For one job which I was desperate to get, I actually practised my lesson with four different classes on the two days prior to my interview. It worked, as I knew exactly where the lesson was up to, and I had time to help pupils who were struggling during the interview lesson.

Your aim has to be to deliver an 'Outstanding' lesson and this is based upon pupils being fully engaged and making good progress which you need to demonstrate. You may not attain this standard but this is what you need to try for. Figure 5.1 gives the criteria for you to consider what Outstanding means in practice.

Table 5.1: Suggested criteria for an Outstanding lesson based on the latest Ofsted guidance

	Teaching	Achievements and Standards	Assessment	Attitudes and Behaviour
Outstanding (1)	Teaching is stimulating, enthusiastic and constantly challenging. Expert knowledge is shown of the subject, how to teach it and how students learn. Methods are well selected and the pace is good. Activities and demands are matched to student needs and abilities. Both partners in a teaching pair reinforce and support learning. Difficult ideas are taught in an inspiring and highly effective way.	Students are engrossed in their work and make considerably better progress than may be expected. They consider difficult ideas and are willing to tackle challenging topics. Achievement is very high.	Work is assessed thoroughly. Feedback clearly indicates how to improve. Q&A and one-to-one in class support checking and developing understanding. Students are helped to judge their own work and set their own targets. Assessment enables students to play a very strong part in making and recognizing improvements in their work.	Students are happy. They are keen to work and take responsibility for their learning. They are helpful, considerate and consistently behave well. They help each other. There are excellent relationships in the classroom.

Adapted from: *Developing a self-evaluating school: A practical guide* by Paul K. Ainsworth

As a middle leader you may wish to go a little further and use the opportunity to show that you have the ability to plan a scheme or module of work. One way of doing this is to take the lesson you have been asked to deliver and design a module with no more than six lessons and probably fewer, showing how you would develop this lesson and/or show what should have come before. This does not mean you prepare lesson plans for each of these lessons but instead show the medium-term planning for the module.

Be prepared to discuss the merits of the lesson and any of its shortcomings at the formal interview if you are shortlisted. This demonstrates that you are a reflective practitioner looking always to improve your practice and a question about how your lesson went is a common one for interviewers to use. This will be covered in further detail in Chapter 7 (pages 75 to 82).

Golden rules for an interview lesson
- Be clear on the lesson topic and profile of the pupils.
- Carefully structure your lesson and do not omit the plenary if you run out of time.
- Look for ways of demonstrating pupils' progress.
- Use the facilities that are available.
- Practise your lesson at your own school.
- Be ready to discuss the lesson at interview.

Presentation
Probably the second most frequently used task is to deliver a presentation on a set theme. There was a time when presentations were used more than delivering a lesson but this is now not the case. A presentation will be used to look at different skills according to the position that you are applying for. If you are applying for a Head of Department position the interviewers will be focused on the content of your presentation rather than whether you are a highly skilled public speaker. If, however, you are applying for a senior leadership position where part of the job may entail fronting staff meetings or parents' meetings, then the interviewers are looking for a far more polished performance in addition to the content of your presentation.

You may be unsure as to whether you should use a PowerPoint slideshow for your presentation. It takes a highly skilled public speaker to deliver a presentation without any visual aids and the PowerPoint gives your audience a visual reminder of the key points of what you are saying. Presentations should be uncluttered, with fewer rather than more words. It is not good practice to use 'fancy' animations or sounds as these can distract from the content and tone of your presentation.

Many candidates are tempted to read their presentation and if you honestly feel that is the only way that you can deliver it then do so as a last resort. However, it is often far more effective if you have your presentation on postcards which you can refer to during the presentation.

Be careful though, as some presentations lend themselves to a more personal approach, especially if more than one presentation has to be given over more than one day. One colleague, successful at a Deputy Head interview, was actually praised for not using PowerPoint in a second presentation, perhaps because she broke away from the security of a prepared slide script. If observers have sat through five very polished but potentially over-prepared presentations, the refreshing spontaneity and more directly engaging style might win the day.

While few interviewers will time your presentation to the second, it is likely to be seen as a black mark if your presentation is far longer than the time you have been given. In some ways it can be seen as a lack of respect towards your audience.

There can be a temptation to give a presentation which purely discusses an issue and can seem a little abstract. The very best presentations focus on how the issue impacts upon the pupils in the school. One way you can do this is to do some research on the school by reading their Ofsted report and their website and trying to use this information in your presentation. I have seen some presentations which have included pages from the school website in their presentation. You can also give practical examples of small things that you could do which would improve the attainment of the pupils.

It is a good idea to provide a brief written summary which you can distribute as appropriate at the end of your presentation. This ensures that the audience is left with your key points. You can also leave this showing as a final slide while you invite questions from those present.

Golden rules for presentations

◆   Use a simple uncluttered PowerPoint.
◆   Avoid too many slides: for a ten-minute presentation 4–8 slides are plenty.
◆   Try not to read your presentation.
◆   Keep to the time limit.

◆ Use examples from the school in your presentation.
◆ Provide a written summary for your audience.

In-tray exercise
You are most likely to be asked to cover an in-tray exercise as a potential senior leader and this task was included in the assessment for the NPQH (National Professional Qualification for Headship). In-tray exercises are also given to pastoral middle leaders as they may often have a wide range of different issues to solve.

The idea at the centre of an in-tray exercise is that there is not enough time to do every task completely. You have to move through the tasks speedily but do not forget the most important part of any in-tray exercise is to ensure you read the scenarios properly and that you answer the tasks set, not the ones you presume are there.

At the beginning of the task be clear about how the interviewers wish the task to be answered. Do they want you to prioritize the tasks or are you only required to suggest how you would solve the problems before you?

One common error that candidates make is in believing that they have to solve every problem in the in-tray exercise themselves. You should also be looking for examples within the in-tray exercise where you delegate some of the tasks; there will be some tasks that need passing to a more senior member of staff too.

Ensure that you record clearly and legibly what you would do with each task in the in-tray. This is one of the few times that your writing will be assessed in the interview process. If you are concerned about your grammar, then using bullet points may be the best solution.

There can be a belief that in every in-tray exercise there must be a disaster that must be acted on immediately, such as an issue related to the Health and Safety of pupils which would mean the closure of the school. This is not always so and be careful before you suggest taking extreme action. There is no reason why you cannot suggest discussing the issue with other key staff and in this day and age you can normally contact absent senior staff by mobile phone.

The best in-tray exercise will be closely linked to the responsibilities of the job which you are applying for. However, this is not always the case and sometimes in-tray exercises can feel a little random to a candidate. This is not for you to worry about; you just need to do the best you can.

Golden rules for in-tray exercises
◆ Read the tasks carefully.

◆ Be clear on how the tasks are required to be answered.
◆ Do not be afraid to delegate tasks or seek further advice.
◆ Be clear about how you suggest prioritizing tasks.

Panel interviews

In addition to the formal interview that normally occurs at the end of the interview process, you may find that you participate in other smaller interviews that are not with the Headteacher. You could be interviewed by a group or groups of middle leaders and it is not uncommon for the school council to interview Headteacher or Deputy Headteacher candidates. If the school has a community dimension with youth workers on site they may also run an interview.

The advice that is given in the next two chapters will be pertinent to these interviews. In addition one of the most important things to remember about these interviews is to keep them in proportion. One of these interviews will not give you the job nor will it prevent you from getting the job.

You need to be aware that some of the interview panels will have their own agenda which is not the same as that of the key decision makers. You need to treat your interviewers with respect but not to be too worried if some of the questioning seems unusual at times! Pupils may ask you something completely random: one candidate was memorably asked what biscuit they would compare themselves to. Middle leaders may want to implicitly criticize a decision by the school leadership.

Golden rules for panel interviews
◆ Do not allow yourself to be too demoralized or excessively encouraged by individual interviews.
◆ Treat your interviewers with respect.
◆ Expect to receive some unusual questions.

Discussion tasks

Probably everybody finds discussion tasks a very strange experience and the alternate title of a goldfish bowl discussion highlights this. A discussion task is where the interviewer sets a topic and the candidates have to discuss the issue with the aim of reaching some kind of agreement or consensus while the interviewers observe. Sometimes discussion tasks have a chair nominated and each of the candidates has to lead the discussion in turn and then highlight the conclusion which has been reached.

There are occasions when you are on interview and one of the candidates sees this type of exercise as an opportunity to score points off the other candidates. This is rarely an effective strategy as interviewers hope that this exercise will allow them to see how you work with other people. The reverse can also happen where a group of candidates are all too nice to each other and as a result no real discussion ensues at all.

One strategy that is often seen as being favourable is to make a point and then ask a certain candidate what their view on the statement is. A second strategy is to begin by suggesting what you agree with in the previous speaker's points and then expand on these.

If you are chairing the group it is even more important to try to ensure that everyone in the group adds to the discussion. It can be tempting to almost enter into verbal tennis, where one person makes a point, you make a point and then rally it back to another person. A better strategy is for you not to make a point in between but instead steer the conversation onto another candidate. You must summarize the discussion at a certain point and check your colleagues agree with the conclusion. If the discussion seems to be flagging, it is the time to add your views.

Remember, though, that most people find this task a very surreal experience. Your main objective is to make some positive points without being seen to dominate proceedings and to show that you can work as part of a team but that you are prepared to defend your points of view articulately and respectfully.

Golden rules for discussion tasks
◆ Do not try to 'score points'.
◆ Do not try to dominate proceedings.
◆ Encourage others to speak.
◆ Be positive.
◆ Be aware that active listening skills are as important as speaking skills.
◆ Be sure your body language is positive.

Other tasks
You may face other tasks during an interview, especially at a senior leadership level. Some schools will ask you to take a psychometric test which is designed to suggest how you behave in certain scenarios. Schools will often be using this to see if it triangulates with other evidence from the day/s. The best strategy is to try not to think about these exercises too much and to give your natural honest answer.

You may be asked to complete a piece of analysis such as looking at the RAISEonline data and reporting what this source of information tells you about the school. You may also be shown the school's budget and asked what challenges face the school in the next few years.

You may be asked to observe a lesson and give feedback to the teacher who delivered it or to comment on the quality of the lesson with an expert from the local authority.

Informal selection tasks

You must remember that in between formal tasks the school is making a judgement on you. This can range from the way you drive into the school car park, how you greet the school receptionist, to the way you engage in conversation at lunch or break time.

You will usually be given a tour of a school and this may be conducted by some pupils. Pupils will often give you an honest perspective of the school but they are also likely to be very protective of the school. It can be a good idea to have some set questions ready to ask the pupils if the conversation is starting to flag. These could include:

- What do you like best about the school?
- What is your favourite subject?
- What would you like to change about the school?
- Are there areas of the school which feel unsafe?

In many schools the pupils will be asked their opinion about the candidates. Pupils do not expect you to be their friend, most pupils respect some distance between you and them but they will want you to be interested in their views.

In some schools the senior member of staff running the interview will encourage the staff to come and see them if they have opinions on any of the candidates. This may also be done informally when a senior teacher asks colleagues if they have any views on the candidates. I always ask my administration staff if they have any comments on the candidates and they regularly give me very perceptive comments.

There is no doubt that you are on show for the whole day. There is a place for many types of teacher in a school. Often it is the candidates who although enthusiastic about the school also show a little bit of reserve that are the more successful candidates. Unfortunately teachers who are at the beginning of their career and desperate to do well may go slightly over the top in such circumstances.

Final thoughts

You need to see all these tasks as positive as they give you an opportunity to show the school what you can actually do. There will be some sections in which you are stronger than others but that will be the same for all the candidates. It is also important that your skill set is the right one for the school. It is no good being the most creative teacher in the world if what the school needs is somebody with iron discipline and the reverse may also be true where a school has a very nurturing, pupil-centred ethos.

You also want to get a job that you can do, so if the pupils do not respond to your lesson, it may be that your style would not work with these pupils. If you are given a task that you cannot do, it may be that mastery of that task is very important for the school at this point in its development and you would struggle in the job.

Finally, I find most interviewers want you to do well on the day/s. The range of tasks is not organized to catch you out; rather they are trying to capture as rounded a view of you as possible.

Key points

1   Delivering a lesson can be one of the most crucial parts of the process.
2   Try to make presentations relevant to the school.
3   Always read all tasks carefully and give the answer they are looking for – not the one you want to give.
4   You are always on interview, be respectful and considerate to all the people you meet.

How to prepare for your interview

The basics

It is likely that one of your major concerns about getting your ideal teaching job is how you perform in the formal interview. You may be anxious about teaching a lesson during the interview day but at least you are always aware that you are trained to teach and that is what you do at your own school, whereas attending an interview can be outside many teachers' comfort zones. Many teachers can be frustrated that their performance in the interview decides whether they are offered a teaching job and may rationalize that interview performance has nothing in common with being able to teach 30 excited 5-year-olds or a class of year 11 students. This may be the case but unfortunately being interviewed is one hurdle that we all face in our desire to obtain our ideal job.

The good news is that there is no doubt that everybody can improve their performance at interview. An extreme example of this is that in televised prime ministerial debates, which occurred for the first time in 2010, it is widely accepted that the candidates spent considerable time practising for something that, in effect, was a glorified job interview. As viewers we could watch how they changed their styles and their effectiveness ebbed and flowed. Similarly, we would probably smile if a student informed us that they could not revise for an examination and the same is true in that we can always practise for an interview.

It is important to remember that few school senior leaders have been trained in how to conduct job interviews and as a result it is much more pleasant for them to interview teachers who have prepared for an interview. If you have made the effort to prepare properly, your answers will be much smoother and the interviewer will enjoy listening to your answers.

In this chapter we will look at different preparation strategies with the aim of developing your skill to present the best of yourself at interview. This chapter will look at how you research the school in greater detail so that you can frame your answers, how you can summarize why you are the best person for the job, what are the key aspects that an interviewer is looking for and finally how you can structure your answers to certain interview questions. These ideas will be developed in the next two chapters when general interview questions are looked at and how you physically present yourself at interview is covered.

Identifying your starting point

◆ Have you previously prepared for interviews?
◆ How effective has this been?
◆ How do you feel about attending an interview?
◆ Are there specific elements of an interview that you wish to improve?

The detail

The three killer questions

All job interviews and selection processes are now constructed around three key questions:

◆ Can you do the job?
◆ Will you do the job?
◆ Will you fit in?

The peculiarity of these is that they will be three questions which are unlikely to be ever asked by an interviewer. While preparing for an interview you need to keep these in mind as all the time you are looking to communicate evidence about yourself that shows a positive answer can be given to the three.

You have already moved some way to answering the first question; can you do the job? In your application you will have given lots of evidence that shows you can do the job and in interview the school is looking for proof that what you have said in your application is true. In preparing for your interview you need to concentrate on having that evidence at your fingertips.

The second question concerns more your motivation for the job and the school. Many Headteachers and senior leaders will have been scarred by the appointment of a teacher who on paper and at interview showed they had the skills for the role but when they began work did not translate this into practice. School leaders will know that signs to indicate whether someone really wants to do the job can only be gathered during the selection days. To answer this question you need to consider why you are applying for *this* job at *this* school and again have this information available with the aim of trying include it in various answers over the day.

There are always some candidates who definitely have the skills to do the job and have the motivation to do the job but they just do not fit in with either the school's or the department's ethos. This can be a considerable dilemma for interviewers as they weigh up whether it is worth taking the risk of appointing an individual who will not necessarily fit in but will be a strong teacher. In this situation the school may be prepared to take the risk but as the seniority of the position increases, schools are less likely to take this decision. Interviewers will gather evidence on how you fit in at many points during the interview procedure as this may be based on how you act rather than what you say during formal interviews. You need to be finding out what the school really prides itself on and then ensuring that you do fit in with this style of working. If you recognize that your way of working is very different from the school you need to ask yourself the question whether this is the right school for you, rather than be appointed and find yourself fighting against an ingrained school culture that does not suit you.

Researching the school

Hopefully you will have researched the school when you wrote your letter of application. However, now that you have received the offer of an interview you need to return to your research and look at the school in more detail. There is so much information available on all schools that with careful study you will gather some very useful thoughts. Later in this chapter we will look at how you can structure this information for an interview answer.

The starting place for your research is the notes that school distributed with the job details. Some schools will helpfully communicate the intended next stages of their development whether at a whole school level for senior leadership appointment or at a Key Stage or department level for teachers and middle leaders. You need to study the development areas and consider which of them you have an interest – or even better expertise – in? It could be that a school states they wish to develop Assessing Pupils' Progress (APP). You then need to think of different examples where you have worked on APP so that you are ready to communicate this to an interviewer.

If the school does not helpfully provide you with the information on their development plans then you have to try to discover these yourself. The next place to look is the Ofsted website for the school's most recent report. In the report will be information on what the inspectors felt were the most important development items for the school. Again you need to study these aspects and consider where your strengths lie. You need to be sensitive in communicating this information at interview as the school may feel the Ofsted inspectors were unduly harsh in their judgement or the school may have tackled such issues head on and now perhaps feel that they have dealt with the matter. It is also worth considering which strengths have been indicated and see if these match yours. If you can highlight these similarities in an interview you are showing the school that you will fit in.

The school may send you their performance data whether this is Key Stage 2, 4 or 5 data. For classroom teachers or middle leaders you will be looking at the data for your specialism and seeing how this compares to the rest of the school. If the results are lower than the rest of the school then you need to be considering what strategies you have used to raise attainment in the past and ideas for the future. If the data is very high in your area, you should be considering how you feel best suited to working in such an aspirational area. As a senior leader you will also be looking for weaknesses in areas of the schools and suggesting how you would intervene to change this situation. You also may be considering ideas which would raise the attainment levels across the school. In both situations you do have to be sensitive as to whether there were reasons that the school may be touchy about. In one interview I highlighted a weakness in Science as an area which needed addressing only to find an internal candidate was heavily involved in that subject area and the governors were not receptive to my comments!

If the school does not send performance data you can still look at that available on different websites such as the DfE or the BBC. However, the data here is more general and may not help you unpick the school's performance in different areas. You may find that a search of the school's website may provide the breakdown that you are looking for.

This leads nicely on to the next stage of your research, which is a wider look at the school's website. You are likely to find a re-iteration of a school's values and vision. Drawing upon this information when you are in an interview by highlighting the match between your skills and the school's ethos is a particularly strong technique. The school's website will also indicate areas where the school is particularly strong such as in the arts or sports. If you have these skills then it indicates you will fit in with the school. The alternative is that if your skills are different you could propose this will add to the education already available at the school.

Golden rules for research

♦ Identify the areas the school states they wish to improve upon and link them to your strengths.
♦ Consider the Ofsted areas for development and think of how you could solve these issues.
♦ Analyse the performance data looking for weaknesses.
♦ Study the school website so you match your profile to the publicized ethos.

What is your unique selling point?

Once you have conducted your research you will have range of information and this can be compared with study notes for an examination. This information will be invaluable in helping you with the interview questions that you face.

Before you start looking at further questions, one of the best pieces of preparation that you could do is to identify your unique selling point, or in terms slightly less strong, can you write in less than 100 words why you are the person for the job?

If you find that question too daunting, to begin with break it down into smaller questions:

♦ What can I offer which makes me different from other candidates?
♦ What makes me fit into this school better than the other candidates?
♦ What special skills or competences have I got which means I can do this job?

Do not worry if on paper your feel that your answers look arrogant. It is your right to be confident and express why you are right for this job. Interviewers are looking for your views on why you are the right person; it is a lot easier listening to you present them rather than having to extrapolate this information from your other answers.

This short paragraph can be so useful to you at varying points in the interview. You can use it to give you confidence before you begin a task, it can be your last minute revision before beginning an interview or it could be the perfect answer to an interview question. Template 6 will give you an opportunity to develop this paragraph.

If you want to develop this idea a stage further why not see if you can summarize this to a mere 30 words so you have one statement. This will make you think very carefully as to why the school should give you the job. You need to be asking yourself what do you have which will make the school more effective? This is not an easy task but it is a fascinating one to work on in the days before your interview. Finally, you may even choose to use it at the end of an interview to remind the interviewers why they should give you the job! This is a brave technique but many candidates and recruitment specialists are convinced of its effectiveness.

Practising questions

There is no short cut for practising interview questions and hopefully the ones in the pages ahead (Chapters 7, 9, 10 and 11) will give you that opportunity. If you have a list of questions you can read them through and think about how you would answer them for this job. You may decide that while this gets you into the thought pattern of interviews, you do not remember the good ideas that you have at that time.

An alternative technique is that which you may have suggested to pupils for revision. Use a set of postcards and write a question on one side of the card and put your answer notes on the other side. One Principal once told me that this method was her secret of interview success. After a number of unsuccessful attempts she committed herself to 'postcard' preparation and was appointed to the next Headship she was interviewed for.

To develop this idea a stage further it can be a good idea to place the questions in two groups, those which you need to answer with a particular relevance to the school and those which are generic questions. For those relevant to a specific job you can spend time prior to the interview writing answers particularly relevant for that school. Those for generic questions you can use more than once, but make sure you keep them up to date. If you choose two colours of cards you can then separate and file the school-specific cards easily after use.

A more high-tech method would be to record individual questions as sound files on a MP3 player, your phone or an ipod. You can then use the shuffle function on a player so that you are asked questions at random and attempt to answer them that way.

When writing answers to interview questions, it can be a good idea to write your thoughts as bullet points rather than as continuous prose. This means when you are reading through your answers you concentrate on the main points.

If you do decide to make notes on cards or something similar, why not take them with you to your interview to look through while you are waiting? I have seen colleagues applying for Headteacher positions doing this and it can be a good way of using such time.

You may be fortunate enough to have a trusted colleague or former colleague to take you through a mock interview. Your Headteacher or another senior colleague may offer to do this for you and you almost feel as though you have to take up such an offer but it can be a very strange experience saying why you would like another job to your current employer. In such circumstances it may be better to take some questions to this colleague and ask them how they would answer the questions if they were in your position. If you do wish to have mock interview you might find the process easier with an advisor from your local authority.

Structuring your answers

The style of questions has changed over time in interviews. One type of question which is used much more frequently is the 'situation' type question. These often begin with phrases such as 'Can you give an example when you have ...' or 'Can you describe a situation where ...'

There are a number of formats which you can use the help you to answer such questions. One framework is the B a STAR model, the acronym formed from the initial letters of the following words:

◆ Benefit
◆ Situation
◆ Task
◆ Action
◆ Results

In many ways you begin this question in reverse by agreeing with the interviewer and stating why you think this issue is important in schools and the **benefit** to pupils. The second stage of the question is to think of a **situation** where you have worked on this issue. You are looking to paint a picture which is negative or dark at the beginning so there is a good reason for you wanting to make a change. The third stage is to translate this reason for change to an easily understood **task.** Be very clear in explaining this to the interviewer so that they

Figure 6.1: B a STAR

B a STAR

Can you give an example of how you have worked in a team?

Benefit: I have enjoyed working in a number of teams, whether my year team or my department and I think it is important that teams of staff have a shared understanding or aim, as pupils appreciate consistency. One example of this is the team I worked on looking at pupil behaviour in my school this year.

Situation: In the winter term there was beginning to be a problem with pupil behaviour in the school and many teachers, particularly new ones, were finding that the behavioural management system was not working properly. I found in my own lessons that I often had pupils coming from another lesson indignant about the way teachers had used the system and as a result it was taking longer to get the pupils settled to begin learning.

Task: Through a staff meeting we agreed to form a small working party which would look at the behavioural management system which was currently in use. The group of eight included a range of staff chaired by a senior leader.

Action: We conducted a range of analyses and I was given the role of conducting the pupil focus groups to discover their opinions of the behaviour management system and collect suggestions on how we could improve it. As a group we shared our findings. We found that it didn't appear to be the system at fault but more the variation in how staff used it. We decided to use part of a training day after Christmas to re-launch the system. I was given the role of presenting the pupil views to the staff and created a short film from the pupil focus group.

Result: After the training day staff seemed to use the system more consistently and I certainly found that the pupils were more settled when they arrived at my lesson. I also found it fascinating giving a presentation to the whole staff as this was the first time I'd done it. I am working on another training session for a twilight workshop on using writing frames.

understand your rationale, why does something need doing? Next is the more personal section with the answer, what **actions** have you or your team taken? Do not feel that you have to take all the credit for yourself, it can be very positive to explain your role if it was a team effort. The last stage is to discuss the success of the project and what the **results** have been. If these results can be translated into pupils' progress, even better. Template 7 will give you the opportunity to practise framing B a Star answers.

You may find there are a small number of projects that you have been involved in which allow you use this technique. If so write the projects down and then you may find that you can apply them to different questions. In one interview you may be asked for an example where you have worked successfully in a team and in another you may be asked for views on improving school behaviour and you can then give the same example of your involvement a working party to develop a behavioural management system.

Final thoughts

You will receive a wide range of advice on how to prepare for interviews and it is apparent that if you do invest time thinking about how you perform in interviews you can make the experience more positive for you and the employer. The starting point is to thoroughly research the school and look for the links between your skills and attributes and where the school needs to improve. A unique selling point phrase can be a good way of highlighting this information.

Strong applicants will spend time practising interview questions. You can do this on your own or you may find that there are others who can also help. You may find that the most effective way of doing this is to build up a set of interview with questions and answers which you can continue to refine if you are not immediately successful. Some types of interview questions lend themselves to a framed response and one such method is known as 'B a Star'. To get the most out of this system, though, you do need to practise it in advance.

Key points

1   Aim to link your research with the three killer questions.
2   Spend time trying to succinctly explain your unique selling point.
3   Develop a systematic way in which you prepare for interview questions.
4   Practise the 'B a Star' technique for answering 'situation' interview questions.

A general guide to interviews

The basics

The previous chapter considered how you could prepare for interviews by focusing on how you can research a school, consider your selling points and structure certain types of answer. This chapter now begins to look at some of the questions you will be asked in a formal interview. You will tend to find that whatever the hierarchical level of the job there will be certain questions that may appear in any interview.

First, this chapter will look at how an interview may be structured. This chapter looks at those questions and gives some hints on how you may wish to tackle the questions. The three chapters within Section Two (pages 89 to 146) will be more specific about answers to the questions and how certain candidates may answer them.

By the end of this chapter you will have a growing awareness of what is expected in a teaching interview and have begun to build up techniques on how you can answer the questions. When you are in an interview and are asked questions that you have heard before this is boost to your confidence and will mean that you can settle into the interview and give the best possible account of yourself. You may want to begin making a set of cards where you can write your answers to the questions in this chapter that you can then keep as a reference while you are waiting to be interviewed.

Identifying your starting point
◆ What structure have you noticed or been told of at other interviews?
◆ Did there appear to be a pattern to the questions you or others have been asked at interview?
◆ Are there questions that you would expect at any interview?

The detail

Structure of an interview

If you are applying for a classroom teaching position or a middle leadership post you will generally find that there is one formal interview within the selection process. If there are a number of applicants this will often occur in the afternoon, once the morning has been taken up with meeting staff, a tour of the school and some type of task. Such formal interviews tend to be between 30 and 45 minutes long depending on the number of candidates that is being interviewed. This means that you are probably looking at only about eight to ten questions, especially if any of your answers promote a discussion. Some teachers are under the impression that they will be asked exactly the same questions as the other candidates. Instead interviewers are quite within their rights to ask you for more detail or ask an additional question about a detail within your answer.

Most interviewers tend to structure their questions so that you have to answer on a range of topics. You may find that you are asked different questions at each interview that you attend but if you study the questions you will see the link between the subject matter of each within different areas in an interview. The following generic areas are likely to be considered in most interviews:

◆ a general opening question
◆ your impressions of the school
◆ reviewing your performance so far on the selection day
◆ personal questions about your character or career
◆ questions specific to the skills required for the role
◆ child protection question
◆ formal questions.

Within this chapter we will look at a range of questions covering each of these topics with the exceptions of questions specific to the role as this will be considered in Section Two (pages 89 to 146).

Opening questions

The idea of all opening interview questions is to try to put you at your ease so that you are then able to answer the more complex questions with greater clarity. The interviewer is often looking for a link that helps them remember your letter of application. You may hope that the interviewer has learnt your letter of application and remembers the detail about you. The reality is that many Headteachers who conduct a number of interviews will have forgotten why they short-listed you and this is your opportunity to remind them. In many ways opening questions are the open goal which you need to be well prepared for. To continue the sporting metaphor your answer really does need to strike the target. Typical opening questions will include:

◆ Why have you applied for this job?
◆ Tell us about yourself and why you find yourself here?
◆ Why would you like to work at this school?
◆ What makes you suited to this role?

In essence each of the questions above could receive an almost identical answer. So if you can try to cover the answers to each of those questions in one response you are on the right lines. They each require a short, recent history of you. The interviewer is not looking for the story of the last decade of your teaching career or education. Instead they are looking at the last few years. For an ITT student you may wish to make reference to your degree and then why you have chosen to become a teacher. If you are already working as a teacher, they will be interested in your current position and maybe the one before that. You then have to explain why this specific role and school and interest you. Make sure you do talk about the school as otherwise the interviewer may assume you recycle this answer at any teaching interview. Finally explore why you are particularly suited to the role by explaining the specific skills you possess. You do not have to go into great detail on this point as hopefully the later questions will give you the opportunity to explain this more fully.

Your impressions of the school
The next group of questions begins to focus on why you wish to work at this school with the aim of highlighting the candidate who is not just looking for any job but really does want to work at a particular school. The second aim of this type of question is to identify how observant you are and whether you have the skills of analysis. The level of job you are applying for will determine the detail an inter-viewer is looking for and the evidence required. You may be asked questions such as:

◆ What are your perceptions of the school so far?
◆ What are your thoughts on the department?
◆ What have you noticed about the pupils at the school?

- From what you've seen what would you want to change?
- How does the school compare to your expectations?

These questions have two main dangers: the first is being over-critical of the school and the second is being too gushing. The clue to the answer to this question is how the Headteacher introduced the school to you at the start of the day. If the Head gave the impression that they were looking to make lots of changes to the school as they were dissatisfied with its performance then you can perhaps risk being more critical. If the Head was very proud of the school and department then you need to be more positive. In both circumstances it is good to highlight aspects of the school that you have observed during the day. In both circumstances you must also ensure that you highlight some positives and some areas for development. At one interview I attended I noticed that the subject room was really untidy with books and resources scattered everywhere. I commented that it was good to see such a range of resources but that I would like to help the Head of Department with their organization.

Reviewing your performance so far on the selection day

One of the common traits of successful education professionals at all levels is their skill of self-reflection. This is sometimes referred to as the 'reflective practitioner', a phrase coined by the education researcher, Schon. If the interview panel includes people who were not present when you taught your lesson that morning, such as a governor, this is also a method used by the other members of the panel to bring them up to speed. Common questions on this topic include:

- Tell us about your lesson?
- What were the strengths of your lesson?
- What would you change if you were to deliver the lesson again?

One of the errors many teachers make in answering this question is to be overly negative or positive about their performance. Instead think about the lesson observations you will have received in the past. You will often be given feedback with perhaps an equal number of positive and negative points and you should be looking to tackle these questions in a similar way. It is a good idea to spend a moment after you have taught the lessons making a few notes to be ready to answer this question, then you will be prepared for it during the interview.

If you have participated in any other activities prior to the interview you may be asked to reflect on your performance in those too, so again be prepared and try to balance the negatives and positives.

Personal questions

Most interviewers will want to find out a little bit more about your personality and what makes you tick. These questions could be asked in an interview for any field of work. You may be asked:

◆ Where do you see yourself in five years?
◆ What are your main strengths or weaknesses?
◆ What CPD requirements do you have?

These questions do not necessarily have right and wrong answers. You may also find that in one school an answer you give is seen as positive and in another school they do not like the same reply. It would be well worth asking the opinion of people you work with about these questions; the important thing is to be positive in your answers without being overbearing. You may want to be Headteacher in five years but a better answer may be to 'concentrate on having done this job well and in the light of this be looking to see what is the next step'.

Some people comment that a weakness is an overdone strength so good answers to this question can include, 'I sometimes take too much on' or 'I like to make sure everything is perfect'. These are both overdone strengths which can also be seen as positives.

In terms of CPD requirements this links with both questions. Try to think of something that is not at the core of the job you are applying for as this may make the interviewer feel you are not currently able to do the job. Instead try to think of something extra that is linked to the role but not its core purpose.

Child protection questions

Following the tragic deaths of the two schoolgirls at Soham it is now expected that at least one member of the recruitment panel will have completed training in safer recruitment and as a result the interview will include some questions which probe your knowledge of child protection. Questions could include:

◆ Give an example of when you have had safeguarding concerns over a child.
◆ When a child has asked to speak you at the end of a lesson, what have you done?

◆ Tell us about an incident when you have taken action to help protect a child.

These questions are not there to catch you out and you just need to answer them honestly. There are not necessarily right or wrong answers and instead your replies will be contrasted with your references and how you relate to children in the school. If the panel has no concerns from your references or how you have related to children in the school it is unlikely that these questions will be used to decide whether you or another candidate is offered the job.

Rounding off the interview

At the end of any interview there are likely to be some more formal questions which do not form part of the selection process but the first time you have an interview it is easy to be thrown and become flustered by the formality of the questions. You may be asked:

◆ Is there anything you'd like to ask us?
◆ Do you feel you've had the chance to show us your full potential?
◆ Do you feel the process has been fair?
◆ Are you a firm candidate for the post?

You can use the first three questions to give a short pithy summary to thank the interviewers for offering you an interview, how much you've enjoyed visiting school and why you think you would be a good candidate for the post. Many of the questions you consider may be the ones to ask when you are offered the post. The final question does not mean you mean that you have to accept the job if it is offered to you but it is asking whether you still wish to be considered for the post. You can answer this question yes and still turn down the job if you feel what is being offered is not to your liking.

Final thoughts

During your career it is likely that you will attend a range of interviews and you may find that you are asked a question as a potential NQT that you are also asked at your Headship interview! You can greatly increase your confidence and hence your performance at interview by practising the questions that are included in this chapter. It can be a good idea to ask your colleagues how they may answer the questions if they were you too.

Key points

1 Practise the basics of why this job, why this school and why you?
2 At the beginning of the day try to determine how satisfied the Head is with the school and look for evidence of good aspects of the school and its areas for improvement.
3 After you've taught your lessons note down two or three strengths and areas for improvement.
4 When asked personal questions about your character try to be positive without being over-confident.
5 Child protection questions are not there to catch you out, just be honest in your replies.

8 | How to present yourself

The basics

We all make judgements on other people even before they speak, whatever we may say or intend. In the same way when anyone meets a group of strangers there will be some individuals that one is drawn towards and some people where the opposite is true.

No matter how much we say that we are going to operate equal opportunities in the broadest sense, all interviewers instinctively warm to some candidates more than others. This does not mean those candidates will be offered the job, it just means that if the decision between candidates is very close such an individual may have the edge. As interviewers generally work in a panel of three, normally of mixed gender, this instinct will also be diluted.

The central aim of this book is how to give you the best chance at interview of getting that job. Any advantage that you can think of will hopefully give you a greater degree of confidence so that you can answer questions more eloquently and perform tasks more efficiently. You may not necessarily agree with all the recommendations in this chapter as it is probably the most subjective in the book and there is no doubt it does err on the side of conservative caution. If there is advice you disagree with and you can present yourself more effectively then why not ask a trusted colleague for their opinion, especially if they work in a very similar school to the one where you are going for an interview.

This chapter gives advice on your general appearance, your interview outfit and how you can ensure your body language presents you in a positive light and ensures people's first impression of you is a good one.

Finally to present yourself well you need to feel comfortable so if following advice in this chapter makes you feel uncomfortable then it would be better to stick with what seems natural to you in those circumstances.

Identifying your starting point

◆ Do you feel confident when at an interview or first visiting your teaching practice?

◆ Have you ever received feedback on what first impressions you make on fellow professionals?

◆ Are you clear about what you would wear at interview?

◆ Have you considered how your body language can help you at interview?

The detail

General appearance

The first thing we will look at in this chapter is your general appearance when you first walk through the doors of your potential new school or into the Headteacher's office. Nobody is expecting you to be over-confident as you walk into a new school but you need to try to avoid being flustered. So before you get out of your car, why not take a minute to compose yourself, just check yourself in the mirror, and practise a smile. Some people suggest sucking a mint before you leave the car as the peppermint is a homeopathic calming agent and it ensure your breath is fresh for that first impression.

As you walk into the school you will need to be able to easily open the door and sign the visitors' book. One immediate way of becoming flustered is having too many items in your hands, which means that you become all fingers and thumbs over these tasks. Try to only have one item in your hands so that means just one bag. Make sure you have already put your keys, mobile phone or wallet away before you walk into school. If you have carried an umbrella then before you sign in make sure you have put it away.

What to wear

The 'what to wear on interview' question can be a minefield for both men and women; but you can make it very simple. What you have to remember is that the majority of senior leaders are in their 50s and often dress conservatively. Your aim is to try to fit in so that you are immediately seen as one of the team. Let your teaching and interview answers represent you rather than your clothing. Often the easiest thing for both men and women is a trouser suit with a blouse for ladies and a shirt and tie for men.

Such simple advice on clothing is often easily heeded by men but many women will find this too dull and hence reduce their confidence. Whatever you wear as a woman good advice is to make sure it passes two tests: sitting in a low comfy chair or leaning over to help a child. Often comfy chairs in offices can be quite low and you need to make sure that when you sit down you don't reveal a mile of thigh. One female senior leader forgot this advice earlier in one job as she sat on the stage in full school assembly and what had seemed a modest skirt as she walked into school seemed to ride up far too much in front of the school. A similar thing can happen with tops as you lean down to help a child with a lesson and all the pupils have eyes for is your bra. I can remember watching one dull interview lesson with a group of year 9 boys, who sat in rapt silence eager for help as every time the teaching student bent to help them they could see to her belly button.

In terms of jewellery the basic advice is still no earrings for men, a maximum of one per ear for women and no more than one ring per hand for either gender (an engagement and wedding ring on one finger count as one). If you have any tattoos it is often a good idea to cover them. One of my colleagues has large tattoos down to his wrists. He was interviewed on a scorching hot day but kept his sleeves buttoned down for the day. While the Head who interviewed him would not have been offended by tattoos I can think of others who would have immediately placed him lower on the priority list because of this.

It is a good idea to have worn your interview outfit at school before you wear it an interview and then you can check how comfortable it is. A suit tried on in the shop can suddenly seem too tight as you reach up to the whiteboard and we all know that those fantastic new shoes can have crippled you by the time you have completed an hour's walk of a large campus on a cold, rainy day. If your outfit is accidentally too revealing if you wear it in your own school you will certainly know this is the case by the break time!

Body language

There are complete books written about how you can master body language. There is probably an equal number on how you can read body language, a topic made popular on television through the antics of Cal Lightman in *Lie To Me* or Patrick Jane in *The Mentalist*. This next section offers some practical ideas that may make you more comfortable during an interview.

Handshakes

There is no obviously no connection between handshake and personality but a very limp handshake can be off-putting for some interviewers just as many people do not wish to have their hand crushed either. You want to be able to hold the other person's hand but be careful at this point. If you do have a 'bone crusher' grip then practise shaking hands with other people. When you meet somebody for the first time why not shake their hand so you get used to it?

Smiling
No interviewer wishes to be faced with a non-smiling or frowning candidate before them. Indeed your aim is to try to build some rapport with the panel so a nervous smile is actually better than no smile at all. Therefore when you greet each interviewer try to smile at them. The same is true is when individuals begin to address you with their questions. Remember some interviewers will be equally nervous as they ask the questions as you may be answering them. Good interviewers will be trying to put you at ease so if you can smile it makes them feel that they are doing a good job too. There is a difference between smiling professionally and acting the clown so while it is perfectly appropriate to laugh at an interviewer's joke, it is probably best not making your own.

Are you sitting comfortably?
The way you sit at interview, as well as making you feeling more at ease, can make an impression on the interviewers. For men try to avoid the look of pundits on *Match of the Day* with legs far apart and your trousers pulled a little too tight; and no woman wishes to accidentally re-enact the Sharon Stone moment. So instead both genders may be better practising the 'low cross'; this is where you sit with your knees close together and legs crossed at the ankle or shin. Some people will prefer to sit with their knees and feet together. You are looking for a stable position which is unlikely to give you pins and needles.

Eye contact
If you do not make eye contact with your interviewers you can appear insecure at best and possibly evasive which you wish to avoid. If you are being interviewed by a panel then one tactic is to make eye contact with the person asking you the question. When a different person is asking you a question move your body position so that you face them. It can be difficult if you are being interviewed by one person to continue to make eye contact with them as it can sometimes feel like a staring-out contest. One solution is to look at the interviewer's left ear – if they are more than one metre away

they will not be able to tell you are not looking in their eyes. Last, a warning for all men if they are being interviewed by a woman to ensure your eye line remains above your female interviewer's shoulder. Even if you are not looking at your interviewer's chest or legs that is the assumption that some women will make!

Hand/arm movements

When you are being interviewed you need to try to limit your hand and arm movements as this can be off-putting to some interviewers. It is perfectly acceptable to move your hands while you are speaking but you need to try to ensure that such movements are not excessive or cover your face. If you aware that you are someone who does move their arms a lot, then one solution is to entwine your hands in your lap. What you must never do is sit with arms folded as this looks defensive at best.

If you have to give a presentation, what to do with your hands can be even trickier. Some of us put our hands in our pockets but this can be considered unprofessional; if you wear glasses holding them can be a good solution. One colleague I know likes to hold a glass of water but this is not always to be recommended. Holding some postcards can be one solution even if you are not using them as an *aide memoire*.

Props

In the previous section we began to consider props. It can be very tempting at interview to fiddle with things but this can disturb your interviewer's concentration. If you are offered tea or coffee in a formal interview, particularly if it is in a cup on a saucer, it can be a good idea to refuse. First, any saucer will highlight any tremors in your hands and second, if you do accidentally spill any it will be very obvious. Requesting a glass of water can be one response as then you are matching your interviewers in having a drink. I would be tempted to avoid offering to pour any drinks as again any nerves are very noticeable. If you do wear glasses try not to keep taking them on and off. Finally if you have long hair, do not play with it. If this is a habit then the best thing is to tie it back to remove the temptation.

Mirroring

One body language technique is called mirroring and this is where you shadow the actions of your interviewer. This is something that should occur naturally but there is no reason why you cannot make small adjustments to your posture so that your interviewer feels that you are connecting with them. So for example if they lean towards to you, lean in slightly too. If the interviewer is having a drink then take one yourself, even if you do not drink it. Obviously be careful with mirroring as it can quickly look comedic if you take it to extremes. It is something you need to practise so why not have a go and then tell the person what you were doing and see what they think of the idea the next time you are having a conversation with someone, whether in the staff room or the pub.

Final thoughts

It does not matter how well you present yourself at interview if you only give an average interview or teach a lesson that is poor. Your central aim must be to complete the tasks to the best of your ability. Presenting yourself at interview should be a physical reflection of how professional you are. If you present yourself well, you will find that your confidence increases and hence your performance does too. Second, if you present yourself well at interview you will be physically showing that not only do you fit in at the school but you will also be a safe pair of hands. As discussed earlier in this book, interviewers do not like to take risks and appearing to fit in reduces the level of risk the interviewer takes in appointing you.

Key points

1   Take a moment before you walk into the school to settle yourself.
2   Be prepared to dress conservatively for an interview.
3   Take care to smile and make eye contact with your interviewers.
4   Ensure that you are seated comfortably during an interview.
5   Be wary of excessive movements or habits which can distract from your answers.

Section Two: Choosing the Position for You

Becoming a classroom teacher

The basics

The previous eight chapters have presented a whole host of information on the job search process beginning at choosing the school which you feel is best for you and ending with how to present yourself at interview. The majority of teachers who are looking for jobs are those in search of a classroom teacher position also known as a main scale position. This is an un-promoted post with no additional salary to the 'main scale', though there will be some colleagues who are classroom teachers but are on the upper pay scale as a result of a number of years of teaching experience. In a primary school classroom teachers are normally responsible for a year group class, whereas in a secondary school you will be employed to teach one or more specialist subjects, and you will also be likely to be responsible for a form or tutor group.

In small schools classroom teachers may have an additional responsibility but it is unlikely they will receive extra salary as this additional responsibility will not require the leadership of other staff. In larger schools it is unusual for classroom teachers to have additional responsibilities as these will be conducted by middle leaders who will receive TLR (Teaching and Learning Responsibility) points for these tasks.

This chapter looks at the applications of two teachers who are looking to gain their first teaching posts as Newly Qualified Teachers (NQTs). Rachel is looking for a post in a primary school whereas Rhianna is hoping to gain her first post in a secondary school. The chapter will look at their letters of applications which are annotated to show the strengths and weaknesses of the letters. A transcript of the answers which they could give to interview questions is also presented. These are strong answers and you should look at how you could provide responses of a similar depth based on your own experience. Please note that the letters shown are intended to be examples of how a candidate puts a letter together, it would not be a good idea to copy such a letter verbatim!

Identifying your starting point
◆ Have you written a letter of application?
◆ What do you think are the strengths of your application?
◆ How could you improve your application?
◆ What questions might an interviewer ask in relation to your letter?

The detail

Becoming a primary school teacher

Figure 9.1: Functional CV – primary school teacher

Rachel Drew

Personal profile
I am a creative, enthusiastic student teacher with a particular interest in KS2 with the additional ability to teach German. I am looking to gain my first post in a Sussex primary school.

Key achievements
◆ Outstanding lesson observations on first teaching practice for Mathematics lessons
◆ Completed a second teaching practice in a German primary school
◆ I am a member, trainer and assessor for the St John's Ambulance Service
◆ I play the violin to Grade 8 and have led recorder sessions as a volunteer in a primary school

Education
2010–2011   University of East Anglia
            PGCE in Primary Education (German)
2007–2010   University of East Anglia
            BA (Hons) History and German 2nd Class
2005–2007   St Cuthbert's Comprehensive
            A-levels: History (C), German (C), Mathematics (D)
            AS-level: French (E)

Employment history
January/February 2011
Lubeck Primary School
Y1 Class Teaching Practice

October/December 2010
William Rice Primary School
Y6 Class Teaching Practice

2005–2010
The Plough Inn
Waitress and Assistant Chef

Interests
I enjoy volunteering for the St John's Ambulance Service and greatly enjoy training and assessing new members. I have always enjoyed music and play the violin and recorder. I read widely both fiction and modern History.

Figure 9.2: Letter of application – primary school teacher

Dear Mrs Baker

I am very excited about the role of Y5 teacher at your school which is advertised on the Sussex County Website. The ethos of your school greatly appeals to me, as I too believe in 'growing together' and encouraging a positive yet stimulating environment. I am a creative, enthusiastic student teacher with a particular interest in KS2. During my current PGCE course at the University of East Anglia, I have built upon my strong academic background to put theory into practice, planning challenging and stimulating lessons and developing a structured method of formative assessment. It is my firm belief that school should enable children to reach their full potential, fostering an inquisitive, understanding and reflective attitude and preparing them for a full and healthy life and I would aim to develop this ethos in my classroom.

I am relishing the opportunity to teach across the curriculum during my teaching practice. My first practice was based in Y5/6 class in a small rural school in Suffolk and my final teaching practice will be a Y4 class in a large school in

Ipswich. In my first placement I have planned fully-differen-tiated lessons across the curriculum, taking a particular interest in the teaching of the core-curriculum subjects. I believe lessons should engage pupils, and try to stimulate an interest in learning and foster confidence by building upon what children find interesting. For example, I was able to teach Maths through 'detective work' where the children had to solve a murder using their mathematical skills. This proved very popular and became a weekly feature in my Maths group!

I have chosen to specialize in the teaching of modern foreign languages and believe this skill added to my diligent class teaching would make me a real asset to your school. I am currently undertaking an additional 4-week placement in a German school, teaching and observing in a year 1 class and the challenge of teaching German children has been a fascinating one. I would be prepared to use my language skills in both curricular and extra-curricular skill time and to support my colleagues where necessary.

Assessment has been highlighted as one of my particular strengths this year, and I have tried hard to develop a system that records both academic and social/personal achievements. While I recognize the importance of testing and summative assessment, I personally find formative assessment during lessons to be a much more useful reflection of learning, and like to use this as the basis of my planning for future lessons. I believe that reflection is an important part of learning, and have been writing extensive evaluations of both the children's and my own learning in lessons.

It is my belief that children respond best to encouragement and positivity in the classroom, and I think it is important to foster an environment where children feel able to make mistakes. I have always tried to be fair and considerate towards pupils, and believe that to some extent, classroom rules should reflect a partnership between teacher and pupils. My classroom would be a positive, caring environment with high expectations and love of a challenge!

I am a friendly, approachable teacher with a proven enthu-siasm for developing creative lessons. I hope that I would add to the reputation of the school through my creative lessons, caring temperament and sense of humour!

Yours sincerely
Rachel

Interview questions

1. Tell us about yourself and why you find yourself here?

I am currently in between my second and third teaching practice. Normally teaching students at the UEA only have two teaching practices but I had the wonderful experience of spending a second and additional teaching practice in Germany, which was fascinating to see how another European country organized their primary education and it was very challenging to be teaching in another language. My first teaching practice was in a small rural school in Suffolk. I worked with a mixed age years 5 and 6 class which meant that I had to carefully differentiate my lessons as the range of ability was widened by there being two year groups together.

I have always enjoyed working with children and when I was doing my A-levels I volunteered in my local primary to help with music lessons. I chose to study a degree in History because I have always loved the subject and enjoyed combining it with German. While I was studying for my degree I volunteered for the St John's Ambulance and was on duty at student parties and sports fixtures. In my second year I became a trainer and in my final year I was an assessor and these experiences of teaching firmed my view that I wished to be a teacher.

I have always enjoyed studying a range of subjects so decided that being a primary teacher would enable me to deliver this richness. I really believe that primary education is so important in setting the foundations of young people's lives and I am really excited about the opportunity of obtaining my first post. On reading your school website and looking at the Ofsted report I thought your ethos of 'growing together' would be one I could really add to and I am sure I would be a good member of your team.

Thoughts of the interviewer: *This is a brief recap of her training with a good explanation of why she wants to become a teacher. The German section has made me remember her letter. I like the detail she shows in quoting our ethos.*

2. After spending a day in the school why would you like to work here?

I was really interested by your school's key aim of growing together as I believe that just as pupils are always learning, teachers are too. When I have walked around school I have seen a lot of questioning: teachers asking lots of questions of the pupils rather than telling them and also the children being encouraged to ask their own questions and from this I can see that everyone can work together. As an NQT I recognize that even though I have received very positive feedback from my teaching practice I also have a lot to learn, and I am sure that while I could add a lot to your school, I could learn too.

I've noticed that the staff enjoy good relationships and this promotes a really friendly feel to the school. I am sure that I could fit into such a staff room and I could be a valued member of the team.

I am keen to work in a small rural school after my own experience of education as a child and this feeling has been increased from my teaching practice. I think it is important that the staff know all the children in the school whether they are in their class or not and I am sure that I could do that here.

> Thoughts of the interviewer: *She has noticed our focus on questioning but has not recognized the different types of questions we are using but then again she is an NQT. I like her humbleness in recognizing she still has much to learn.*

3. Where do you feel is the place of Modern Foreign Languages in a primary school?

I am aware that the government has removed the compulsion for primary schools to deliver MFL within their curriculum but I still feel it is an important subject to cover for primary children. I find that primary school pupils love to speak in a foreign language; they love the mystery of almost their own secret code. The greater the confidence that primary children can gain with foreign languages the more successful they will be at secondary school in their language lessons.

I also think that learning to speak a foreign language is extremely helpful for their English as they learn about the structure of a language and how it is constructed which can then provoke some good learning points.

I think that languages are not just about delivery in the curriculum time but there is also an opportunity to broaden the extra-curricular provision through a language club. Children can develop their speaking skills, make pen-friends, find out about the country and its culture, and also sing songs and enact drama – experiences that I would have loved as a child, but never had the opportunity.

Thought of the interviewer: *She is aware of the current policy on foreign languages in primary schools. The secret code would definitely appeal to our pupils and I like her ideas for an extra-curricular club.*

4. One of the areas that we are really seeking to develop is our Mathematics provision especially in Key Stage 2. How could you help with this?

As a child I really loved Maths, and I found it quite hard deciding which degree to choose as I was really torn between Maths and History. I am very aware that in Maths teaching so much depends on the creativity and enthusiasm of the teacher. I had a real variety of Maths teachers at secondary school and while I always enjoyed it, I noticed that my friends had a lot more success with one of the creative teachers. It is that creativity that I would be hoping to bring to your Maths lessons. I think that we need to move away from textbooks and work books and instead find ways for children to explore numbers and find patterns. I think one way of doing this is to look for places where Maths can join with other subjects. I always remember being shown the Fibonacci number sequence in nature with photographs of trees and branches and that made Maths come alive to me. During my teaching practice I taught a series of Maths lessons with the aim of solving a murder which the children really enjoyed. So I would hope I would have the opportunity to plan rich Maths lessons, include them in the scheme of work and share these ideas with other teachers.

Thoughts of the interviewer: *Talks about the richness of Mathematics and her lesson idea indicates that she is creative thinker. However, I'm unsure if solving a murder is appropriate for younger children.*

5. Where do you see yourself in five years?

I find that such a hard question and it is something that my parents often ask me. I think that my first aim is to ensure that I am an outstanding teacher. There is so much to learn as a primary teacher as it is not good enough to be extremely competent in just one curriculum area but to have skills in lots of different subjects. If I can develop those skills I hope that I can take on some responsibilities in the future. You mentioned Maths in the earlier questions, so perhaps in a few years time there may be an opportunity to co-ordinate the Maths at the school. I'm also interested in continuing in my studies and perhaps work towards my Masters and maybe in five years I will have gained that. However, probably my biggest aim is to ensure that I am a valued member of this school and that I have helped the school and its pupils to progress as much as possible.

Thoughts of the interviewer: *Good she's not trying to run before she can walk by racing ahead for promoted posts and I'm sure there could be an opportunity for numeracy coordination in the future. I wonder what type of Masters does she mean, the new teaching and learning course or a more traditional one.*

6. How do you feel you could add to the extra-curricular provision at the school?
As I said earlier I'd love to run a language club either based around German, building upon my experiences and contacts from my second teaching practice, or French which I studied at sixth form. I think there is so much that I could do with a language club. The children could practise their speaking and also sing in French or German. We could send tapes to children in a partner school. I don't know if you have video conferencing facilities but that looks a really exciting way of developing links with another school. I'd also like to do some cooking based on France or Germany as the children always love that.

One of my other interests is music and when I was a sixth former I led a recorder group at a local primary school and I would really enjoy the opportunity to do that again.

As a student I've been an active member of the St John's Ambulance and I would like to use my training skills to give children at this school basic first aid skills which they could then build on as they get older.

Thoughts of the interviewer: *It's a shame she hasn't got any sporting interest as we are lacking that at the moment. I wonder if she is aware of that. The language club could be interesting but we haven't got video-conferencing facilities. I can see our older pupils liking a first aid course.*

7. Is there anything you'd like to ask us?
One of the areas which I do want to develop is my PE teaching skills. Would you be able to support me with this?

Thoughts of the interviewer: *I was concerned about this lack of a mention of PE but if she is keen to learn that is good.*

8. Do you feel the process has been fair?
Yes I do. I've really enjoyed the opportunity to talk to so many pupils and to chat with your teachers. I think this is a lovely school and I feel I could add a lot to it. I'm sure my interests in Maths and languages would be helpful.

Thoughts of the interviewer: *She does seem really committed to Maths and languages.*

9. Are you still a firm candidate for the job?
Yes!

Becoming a secondary school teacher

Figure 9.3: Functional CV – secondary school teacher

Rhianna Jones

Personal profile
I am a committed and energetic teacher who is eager to start their career in a successful school which puts the needs of the student first.

Key achievements
◆ International netball player for the last five years.
◆ Level 3 netball coach.
◆ Wide range of sporting skills from team sports to studio exercise classes.
◆ First class degree in Sports Exercise Science from the University of Derby.

Education

2010–2011   University of Loughborough
             PGCE in Physical Education (Secondary)
2007–2010   University of Derby
             BSc (Hons) Sports and Exercise Science, 1st Class
2005–2007   St Michael's Comprehensive
             A-levels: PE (D), Biology (D), Geography (E)
             AS-level: Psychology (E)

Employment history

December/February 2011
City School
First Teaching Practice

2005–2010
Acer Summer Sports Camps
Netball Coach

Interests

My main interest is playing netball for Loughborough Lightning and the Wales national team. I also enjoy aerobics and a variety of studio exercise classes, and play basketball for a mixed recreational team in a university league.

Figure 9.4: Letter of application – secondary school teacher

Dear Mr Summer
I wish to apply for the post of Teacher of Girls' PE at Beech High School. I aspire to work in such a successful and hard working institution as yours and I strongly believe that my experiences in sport and during my education will enable me to make a positive contribution to your school and the Physical Education department. I have a passion for teaching, sport and physical activity in general and thrive on being able to share this with young people and the adults I work with. In line with the job description I firmly believe that providing enjoyment and challenge in PE is essential in promoting students' engagement and achievement both in curriculum and extra-mural time.

My teaching mentors and university tutors have commented positively on my teaching competence and consider that I have a particular strength in developing positive and supportive relationships with the students I teach. I value the contribution that all students can make regardless of their background or current attainment, and work hard to make sure the students are aware of this. Building students' confidence in this way improves their progress and enjoyment while under my care and helps them achieve their full potential.

During my PGCE there has been a strong focus on developing excellent practice. I am a critical and reflective practitioner who always strives to make improvements in whatever I am involved in by accepting feedback from colleagues and outside agencies. My experience in international sport has meant that I have been used to receiving constructive criticism and been expected to apply it quickly to improve my performance. I have been praised for using this skill by mentors during my teaching practice. As an international sports person I am acutely aware of the expectation of being a role model and an ambassador to those around me and I taken this professional approach to my studies. As a team sports player I understand the importance of communication and team work and I am equally comfortable taking a supporting role in a group as well as stepping forward to lead.

During my teaching practice I regularly involve students in activities that challenge them to observe, evaluate, officiate and manage themselves and their peers while developing independent learning skills. Different students have strengths in various roles and activities in PE and one of my key aims is to find the strengths in all young people, engage with them and challenge them to improve further.

My technical skills lie in invasion games, in particular netball and basketball, both of which I play regularly. The physical conditioning that I undertake for my sport has given me a strong understanding of physical skills and body management. I have really enjoyed drawing on this to deliver modules on boxercise, aerobics and dance which have really engaged boys and girls in core Key Stage 4 curriculum time.

My commitment to extra-curricular activities during my teaching placement demonstrates my dedication to supporting students. I have greatly enjoyed running representative school teams as well as social clubs and target group activities.

As a teacher at your school I would endeavour to enforce the school and department policies while also bringing to the job my own enthusiasm and commitment in order to continue the excellent reputation that Beech High currently has. I am keen to work in a successful and motivated department where I can establish my teaching and develop it to its potential.

I look forward to the opportunity to discuss my application with you in person.

Yours sincerely
Rhianna Jones

Interview questions

1. Why do you want to be a teacher?

For as long as I can remember I have enjoyed playing sports. At primary school I would play everything from hockey to football in the playground with the boys. At secondary school I continued to play every team sport that I could. While I was at secondary school one of the PE teachers encouraged me with my netball. She was also the county coach and gave me the opportunity to attend the county trials even though she insisted on another coach selecting players from our school. While I was in sixth form she encouraged me to coach some of the younger children and, with some of the other pupils, I gained level 1 coaching qualifications. At university I concentrated on my own netball but each summer I have worked at a sports summer school. I found that I really enjoyed working with the young people and seeing them improve and from this I started my PGCE. I must admit I was nervous as to whether my motivation would be as effective with older students who were less interested in sport and City school was certainly a challenging first practice. I found, though, that I loved the challenge and teaching those groups of Key Stage 4 pupils made me feel so alive. The opportunity to inspire children to participate in sport is such an honour and it is PE teachers at primary and secondary schools who have a key role in this. I want to give children the same encouragement I was given whether it is to children who are on a weight loss programme or G&T (gifted and talented) children.

Thoughts of the interviewer: *My concern is how effective will she be with less motivated or talented pupils and straight away she is addressing this issue.*

2. Tell us about your lesson. What went well and if you were to do it again what, if anything, would you change?

The lesson was to teach balance to a mixed group of year 8 students. I started the lesson with a warm-up, where the pupils had to move around the hall and when I called 1, 2, 3 or 4 they had to perform a balance with that number of points of contacts on the ground. I found the pupils were enthusiastic and worked hard on the topic. We then discussed the different types of balance so that students understood the language of balance. I gave the students cards with different balances on which they then had to replicate with their group. The balances were at different National Curriculum levels and I encouraged the children to choose balances which challenged them. Finally for the plenary I asked each group to demonstrate a balance and members of the group had to grade it according to a pro forma.

I felt the pupils made really good progress and were engaged in the lesson. I thought the pupils made good progress as they worked through the balances and by the end of the lesson from the pro formas they knew how they could improve their balance work. If I was to do the lesson again I would like to use a whiteboard or projector to show the children different balances. During the starter I would have only used part of the hall. I did do this with the main part of the lesson as I realized the space was quite big.

Thoughts of the interviewer: *Good, my observer had commented about using only part of the hall. I like her comment on the progress the children had made. I wonder if she could give National Curriculum levels to the pupils' work.*

3. Describe a classroom based lesson that you have taught which went particularly well and explain why?

The lesson that I taught last week to a year 10 GCSE PE group was graded as Outstanding by my mentor. I was teaching a lesson on how the body circulates oxygen around the body. We began with a drag and drop starter on the interactive whiteboard where the pupils had to label parts of the body involved in the circulation. The pupils then completed a diagram and stuck this in their books. We watched a short animation on brain pop which explained the theory. I then placed the children into three groups and they had to use drama to illustrate how oxygen is moved around the body. Each group filmed their piece of drama. It was a dry day so we worked outside the classroom and this meant the children had lots of space so they weren't clashing with each other. After 25 minutes we returned to the classroom and the pupils had to complete a short 5-question quiz on what they had learnt in the lesson. In the next lesson I was going to show the films of the three pieces of drama and the children were going to mark them using a pro forma. The children were really motivated by the task and the quiz at the end of the lesson showed they had made progress. I find that GCSE PE children like to do kinaesthetic activities as this mirrors the way they learn during physical activity.

> Thoughts of the interviewer: *This sounds a really good lesson with a wide range of activities. She seems very knowledgeable on ICT; Interactive Whiteboards, Brain Pop and using video cameras.*

4. What do you think are the most important features of a GCSE theory PE lesson?

I think with all lessons the students need to know what they are going to learn during the lesson. You need to use a starter to identify what the children know at the beginning of the lesson and then a plenary at the end so they can see how much progress they've made. As I said before I think it is important to use as many kinaesthetic activities as possible and PE teachers need to be continually looking for fresh ideas to do this. I also think it is important to use ICT, in particular audio-visual clips so that the children are inspired. If I can link the theory to a famous sportsman or woman I think this helps them learn more effectively too.

> Thoughts of the interviewer: *She has a good grasp of classroom based lessons and the link to sportspeople would certainly interest many pupils.*

5. What are your biggest strength and weakness?
I think this is a really hard question and one that is so difficult to answer. I think my biggest strength is my commitment. When I want to do something I always give 100 per cent of myself so whether that is training for my own personal sport, working towards my degree or planning training sessions for a children sports team I really do try to ensure that I give my all. This probably links in with my weakness in that I am perfectionist on my own performance so I'll always want to train more, revise for longer or tweak that lesson plan one last time.

Thoughts of the interviewer: *A strong answer as this isn't really a weakness at all. I wonder how she reacts to people who are less committed than she is.*

6. How do you see your role in contributing to the extra-curricular provision at this school?
I think for PE teachers this is such a key part of our role. If my PE teachers hadn't taken me to fixtures or training I wouldn't have got as much out of PE as I have done. I would hope to have responsibility for at least one team to take them to fixtures. I would also like to run lunchtime and after-school fitness classes. During my teaching practice I enjoyed sharing the teams with other staff; even though you attend more fixtures this way, you can learn a lot from each other.

Thoughts of the interviewer: *Our PE staff take responsibility for more than one team and are usually out at least two after-noons a week, I wonder if she will have the time to do this.*

Supplementary: How will you fit in your extra-curricular commitments with your own sport?
A lot of training relates to personal fitness goals so I tend to get up early in the morning and do an hour's training before school; that's something I've always done. We have one fixture a week and I would hope I would be able to work with the Head of the PE to plan fixtures around this fixed point. I believe that if things are important you can always find a way to manage things and as I said I would be 100 per cent committed to my teaching.

> Thoughts of the interviewer: *This seems reasonable and is less than I would have expected. I need to talk to the Head of PE about how he feels about this.*

7. Is there anything you'd like to ask us?
As you know the Olympics are in London next year. It is every sportsperson's dream to take part. Would you support me with this?

> Thoughts of the interviewer: *It would be amazing to have an Olympian on the staff. Could her fellow team members come into the school? I think we would cope with the cover in this scenario.*

8. Do you feel you have had the opportunity to show us your strengths for this position?
Yes. I really enjoyed teaching the lesson and I was pleased that I was given the opportunity to show you a different sport. I think the pupils at this school have been fantastic, whether those that gave me a tour, were in my lesson or ate with me at lunchtime. They are a real credit to you. I just feel this would be a great school to work in and I am sure that I would be able to really motivate them.

> Thoughts of the interviewer: *That's a nice comment about her children; I'll ask the Head of Year to pass that information on to the children. She does seem very pupil centred and that is one of those attributes we are looking for in this school.*

9. Are you still a firm candidate for the job?
Yes!

Final thoughts

It is not always easy to get a classroom teaching position in your perfect school and one way of achieving this is to use the ideas in the book to write the strongest letter that you can and then to prepare carefully for your interview day. You need to plan the best lesson you can and then practise interview questions.

Key points

1 Personalize your letter for the school.
2 Spend time planning a lesson that fits your personality.
3 Practise answering interview questions.
4 Avoid writing the same letter to different schools. If you use a letter as a template be sure to check and double check you have edited the school's details.

The basics

Middle leaders are the real engine room of school improvement. Some people use sporting parlance to consider them the player managers of the staff room. While they lead groups of staff, they are still predominantly judged on their performance in the classroom due to the number of lessons they deliver.

Middle leaders are paid an additional sum of money in addition to the main scale. This is called Teaching and Learning Responsibility points or a TLR. There has been a considerable change in emphasis from the management points that were in place in schools seven years ago. Previously, management points were allocated for a range of tasks and the teacher did not necessarily have to lead staff; instead they could be responsible for an element of the school which could perhaps be delivered in isolation. With the TLR reform, the emphasis is now on leadership of colleagues and this must be reflected in your application for such a role.

Obtaining a middle leadership post involves a very competitive search. For many teachers it is only the beginning of a journey which will see a few reach the post of Headteachers. Other teachers will stop at various points from second in a department to Deputy Head. Schools are very conscious that they want to get the best candidate in place at a middle leadership level and senior leaders will recognize that they rely on middle leaders to be their expert in certain areas, whether this is a subject co-ordinator in a primary school or curriculum leader in a secondary school.

This chapter looks at the applications of two teachers who are looking to gain a middle leader post. Peter is looking for a post in a prep school as subject co-ordinator whereas Felicity is hoping to become a Head of Year in a secondary school. This chapter presents their letters of application, which are annotated to highlight how they have presented the experience from their CVs. Any potential middle leader will be able to make use of the application whatever phase of school they wish to apply to. A transcript of the answers they would give to interview questions is also included. The answers show good detail with careful presentation of the information. You should try practising the questions and consider using the responses to help frame your answers.

Identifying your starting point
◆ Have you written a letter of application?
◆ What do you think are the strengths of your application?
◆ How could you improve your application?
◆ What questions might an interviewer ask in relation to your letter?

The detail

Becoming a prep school Head of Mathematics

Figure 10.1: Functional CV – prep school Head of Mathematics

Peter Ashworth
Personal profile
I am a high quality primary school practitioner who is looking to specialize in Mathematics by building on my further studies to work with year 3 to year 8 pupils. I have a wide interest in sport ranging from the main team games to outdoor education.

Key achievements
◆ Completed an Advanced Diploma in Mathematics Education.
◆ Article published in the Association of Teacher of Mathematics termly magazine, on teaching algebra using a kinaesthetic approach.
◆ Level 1 cricket coach and the school team won the district quick cricket title.
◆ Hold the Walking Group Leaders Award and lead walks for a ramblers group.

Education
2009–2010   The Open University
                    Advanced Diploma in Mathematics Education

2004–2007	Bishop Grosseteste University College Lincoln
	BA (Hons) Primary Teaching Studies with QTS Status, 2nd Class
2005–2007	Robert Pattinson Secondary School
	A-levels: Mathematics (C), PE (C), Psychology (D)
	AS-level: Art (E)

Employment history

2007 to Present	Haddington All Saints Primary School
	Teacher of Year 5 and Year 6/Key Stage 2 Mathematics Co-ordinator

Interests

I enjoy both playing and watching sport. I am a keen cricketer representing my village team and running the junior section. In the winter I play for Lincoln Thirds Rugby XV. I enjoy walking in the Peak District and leading walks for the Young Ramblers Group.

Figure 10.2: Letter of application – prep school Head of Mathematics

Dear Mr Kent

I am writing this letter in application for the post as Head of Mathematics at St John's Prep School which was advertised in *The Times Educational Supplement*. Your school has such a good reputation in Lincolnshire both academically and from a sporting perspective that I feel my talents would enable me to make a considerable contribution to St John's.

I have been a year 5 and 6 teacher in a large village primary school and have enjoyed teaching across the curriculum. In the last two years I have specialized in Mathematics. I took on the role of Key Stage Mathematics Co-ordinator and in parallel began to study for the Advanced Diploma in Mathematics Education. The opportunity to reflect on how children can learn Mathematics effectively has greatly informed my practice. I considered it important that if I was to properly prepare children for Key Stage 3 Mathematics then

I needed to understand the demands of years 7 to 9. To help me do this I have worked on a team teaching project with a local secondary school and last term I spent half a day week teaching across Key Stage 3. I am sure this will mean that I am well qualified to teach year 7 and year 8 Mathematics at St John's and ensure that the pupils are well prepared for Common Entrance Examinations.

As Head of Mathematics at St John's I would relish the prospect of ensuring that schemes of work are well-prepared and that there is a good range of activities and resources for other teachers to use in their Mathematics teaching. Last year I re-designed the Algebra scheme of work at my primary school. I considered it important that all children met this subject but a range of resources was required to develop the skills of children who hoped to take the 11+ examinations while also enabling children with less developed Mathematical skills to learn alongside them. I found kinaesthetic activities greatly helped some of the less able pupils and they made good progress and I used investigations to stretch the most able. It was a challenge to persuade other teachers to use these lessons. However, once I invited my colleagues to observe my lessons and ensured clear lesson plans were available, they began to use the materials and were delighted with the pupils' learning. Some of these ideas were published in an article for the Association of Teachers of Mathematics. I would hope to develop these ideas further at St John's.

This experience helped develop my leadership skills. I think it is important to be able to show fellow teachers curriculum ideas in practice so that they can see the benefits themselves. It is also necessary to provide carefully prepared written plans so that teachers can concentrate on the delivery of the materials and hence develop their confidence. I recognize it is essential following any feedback from colleagues to be flexible in adapting schemes of work in the light of this.

I also consider the sporting development of pupils important and this is a considerable attraction of working at St John's. I recognize that the main team games of rugby and cricket are an important part of prep school life and I am sure that I could add value to your provision. I am a level 1 cricket coach and currently run the junior section at my cricket club. In recent years I have begun to play rugby for the first time since school and greatly enjoy the experience. I would like to have the prospect of passing my knowledge on to your senior pupils and would be eager to work towards a coaching qualification. I also enjoy outdoor pursuits and hope that with slightly older pupils at St John's I would be able to contribute to residential or day outdoor activities with your pupils.

I am an energetic and conscientious teacher who works hard with initiative, creativeness and as a dedicated team member and whatever I do I wish to give complete commitment whether this is in my classroom practice, my academic studies or leisure activities. I enjoy challenges and I work well under pressure. I have high expectations to teach clearly structured, active and engaging lessons where all children make progress and I would aim to assist other teachers delivering Mathematic to reach this target. I am eager to develop my leadership skills through supporting and coaching my colleagues. My planning and organizational ability will be important in this respect as will my interpersonal skills.

I am looking for a position that will allow me to continue to develop my teaching at all levels, specifically my Mathematics and PE skills. I am looking to build on my leadership experiences and I believe that I could successfully lead the Mathematics department. I am eager to work at St John's with its reputation as a successful school with a clear, forward thinking and positive ethos. I feel my own personal high standards, commitment, passion for teaching and approachable personality would complement your team.

I look forward to the opportunity to present myself for interview at your school.

Yours sincerely

Peter Ashworth

Interview questions
1. Why would you like to work at this school?
It's strange, but I recently said to one of my friends that I'd love to work at St John's and then I saw the advertisement for this post.

You have a great reputation in the county for the care that is given to the children and how this is impacts on their academic and wider development. I think the view that it is the whole child that we are educating that is so important.

Even though I have qualified as a primary teacher, I do enjoy working with the older pupils and your age range of 5–13 as a prep school would give me the opportunity to teach with such pupils while still working with the younger pupils too. I am really interested in working in an independent school as my friends who do so always say that you concentrate on the teaching and the smaller class sizes give you the opportunity to really get to know the pupils not only in your class but across the school.

I am looking to develop my Mathematics and my leadership skills and I think this role is an ideal opportunity to allow me to do this. I am also passionate about my sport so it would be great to take the under-11s or under-13s rugby team to fixtures in the winter and then really work on their cricket skills in the summer months.

I am really impressed by your school as I've been shown round this morning. Everyone seems so happy but also working really hard. It really does seem as good as I have been told and I would love to come and work at your school.

> Thoughts of the interviewer: *Candidate seems to have a rounded view of education and keen to work at this school.*

2. What would your immediate task be in developing the department?
One of the things that appears to be lacking at the moment is a formal scheme of work and this must make it difficult for other colleagues who also teach Maths lessons. There is a good set of textbooks but without a scheme of work, it can be easy to rely on the textbooks and work through them page by page and miss the opportunity to enrich the curriculum.

My first task would to be look at the resources in the department and consider how effective they are in providing coverage of the Common Entrance Exam at 13 and the 11+ exams that some children will sit. This would then enable me to prepare long-term and medium-term sections of the scheme of work.

Once I'd done that I'd focus on developing short-term plans for the areas of the curriculum that the textbooks do not deal with as well as I think they could do.

I'd also want to ensure the two Maths rooms are as welcoming as other areas of the school. There are some fantastic displays in many areas of the school and those rooms must be good for the children to work in. I'd look to quickly display the children's work and also provide displays which ask the children questions, becoming a teaching resource as well as decoration.

> Thoughts of the interviewer: *He's right, I've been concerned about these things for a while, the curriculum has been a little stale and this is reflected in the area but I wonder what the other teachers will think of his views.*

3. How do you work with colleagues to develop the curriculum?
It is easiest for me to answer this question by talking about when I have worked with my colleagues. I think one of the only ways of ensuring that a department uses a scheme of work or curriculum is to work with the other teachers so that they have a sense of ownership for the curriculum and feel comfortable with scheme.

When I became Key Stage Maths Co-ordinator I recognized that there was very good teaching of aspects of mental Maths and this could be seen through the children's performance in that section of the Key Stage 2 examination paper but particular for the most able children their performance in the algebra and patterns section of the paper was not as good and this was reducing the number of level 5s for our school.

This gave me a reason for developing the curriculum and I shared this with the other teachers who taught year 5 and year 6 Maths. After all, many teachers are happy with the adage, if it ain't broke, don't fix it. Once the teachers recognized there was an issue with this element of the curriculum they were happy to see it changed. In discussing this with the teachers it was apparent that in some ways they were a little scared of teaching algebra and patterns as they saw this as a secondary school issue. We did share our ideas of how we thought we could teach this.

I planned two short schemes of work for year 5 and year 6 incorporating ideas from each teacher and tested them with my own classes. The pupils were receptive. So I then offered to team teach some of the lessons with the other teacher. The Head offered to cover my lessons while I did this.

The lessons went well and the teachers said they would work through the rest of the module with their classes. When we studied the Key Stage 2 results in the autumn term following we were really pleased to see that the percentage of level 5s had increased by 10 per cent.

Thoughts of the interviewer: *The other candidates have given a theoretical answer to this so it's good to hear something very practical with a positive outcome. I'm not sure if my teachers will be receptive to team teaching though!*

4. How do you see the role of calculators in primary Maths?
I see that one of my key roles in teaching primary pupils is to ensure that they have good mental strategies for performing calculations. If they don't have a good knowledge of times tables or addition and subtraction it can be so difficult to look at other topics like angles or algebra. The only way of doing this is to give the pupils lots of practice at mental calculations.

However, at the same time there are lots of good lessons where you can use calculators which can help children with their Mathematics and it is also true that by the time pupils are studying towards Key Stage 3 Mathematics they need to have developed the skills to recognize when is the right time to use a calculator and when isn't. So we need to give children opportunities to use calculators in primary school to help with this process.

As with many things in teaching it is about finding a balance.

Thoughts of the interviewer: *I'm happy with this answer. I would have been interested to hear examples of primary lessons that do use calculators though and also at what age he thinks the children should start using calculators.*

5. Can you give an example of when you have successfully dealt with a demanding parent?
I imagine that working successfully with parents at an independent school is so vital as parents have to feel even happier with their choice of school if they are paying directly for the education.

Earlier this year, I had a complaint from one child's parent that the child was being bullied at break time. I think the important thing is often to just listen to the parent as if it involves their child being very upset they are upset too. One of the things that I have found is that if I try to solve the issue there and then it is less effective. So in this situation I said that I would talk to their child and try to find out a little bit more what the problem. The parents were bothered about their child at break time so I said that I would give their child a task to do with another child at the break time. The parents were still not happy with this as they wanted the 'bully' punished.

When I spoke to the child later that day about the incident it sounded like they had fallen out with one of their friends. I made sure I saw the parent at the end of the day to say how their child had been happier today and the child also said they'd enjoyed break time. Again the parent wasn't a 100 per cent happy as no-one had been punished but they were less demanding as the child was happier. I said I would continue to monitor the situation and if they had any more concerns to please send a note with their child the next day in case I was unable to take a phone call.

> Thoughts of the interviewer: *I'm pleased he's realized that we do have some demanding parents. My concern with this answer is that he wants to solve the problem himself and I would like to know of any potentially unhappy parents.*

6. How would you contribute to the wider ethos of the school?
As I wrote in my letter, I'm really keen to become involved in the sporting side of the school and would help where ever I could be most assistance to the school. My favourite sports are Cricket and Rugby and I would like to take practices and fixtures but if you need me to take a different team then I would be happy to help with that.

I know you do a residential trip with year 8 and I would be happy to help if I could as I have the Walking Group Leaders Award but I also understand if there are already staff who normally go on that activity.

I just think it is so important that children have the opportunity to take part in sport and I also think for teachers it is a good way to form relationships with the pupils.

> Thoughts of the interviewer: *This looks good as I'm looking for another good sports coach. My PE teacher would be glad of some help here too.*

7. Is there anything you'd like to ask us?

As you know from my letter I do not have a rugby coaching qualification but I have played a lot of rugby. Would I be able to coach the pupils or would you expect me to have obtained my level 1 coaching award before I start at the school?

Thoughts of the interviewer: *We've not usually bothered about this in the past but it would be good if he could organize his certificate prior to starting.*

8. Are you still a firm candidate for the job?

Yes, I would really like the opportunity to work at your school. I am sure I would be able to help with the development of Maths and sport at St John's.

Becoming a Head of Year

Figure 10.3: Functional CV – Head of Year

Felicity Short
Personal profile
I am an enthusiastic and organized energetic teacher looking to use my strong communication skills to inspire pupils and tutors as a Head of Year.

Key achievements
◆ Developed a tutorial programme for year 12 and year 13 students.
◆ Introduced GCSE Design Technology (Resistant Materials) and all the students achieved Grade C and above.
◆ Led a group of pupils to the Gambia for a school building programme.
◆ Elected by the teaching staff as a Teacher Governor.

Education
2003–2006   Nottingham Trent University
             BA (Hons) Secondary Design and Technology
             Education 2nd Class
2005–2007   St Peter's Comprehensive
             A-levels: Design Technology (B), ICT (D),
             General Studies (D)
             AS-level: Art (C)

Employment history

2009–Present   Assistant Head of Sixth Form, St Olave's
2007–2009   Teacher of Design Technology, St Olave's
2006–2007   Volunteered as Teacher of English in the Gambia

Interests

I am a Guider and lead a Guide Unit and assist at a Ranger Unit. I enjoy travelling and have a particular interest in African culture

Figure 10.4: Letter of application – Head of Year

Dear Miss Grace

I note that you currently have two separate advertisements in *The Times Educational Supplement* for a Head of Year and a Teacher of Design Technology. I am an experienced Technology teacher who is currently an assistant Head of Year and I believe by combining the two posts I could make a strong contribution to your exciting and rapidly improving school.

After qualifying as a Design Technology teacher I had the wonderful experience of being able to establish a Resistant Material course at St Olave's. In the first year of examination, I was extremely proud that all the students achieved a grade C and above. The following year the school received an Ofsted inspection and I was observed teaching Key Stage 4 Resistant Materials and my lessons were described as Good with some Outstanding features.

I base my teaching philosophy on considering all of my students as individuals with very different talents. Some students have very strong design skills whereas others have an aptitude for realizing their ideas. By recognizing this variation within my classes I can understand how best they can acquire knowledge and skills and adapt my teaching style to meet their needs. At the same time I am constantly monitoring their progress and providing extra support when they fall behind with the aim of ensuring all the students achieve their potential.

Participating in a school working group discussing Learn 2 Learn and Building Learning Power has ensured that I continually develop my teaching practice and assessment methods.

In my role as Assistant Head of Sixth Form, I am responsible for looking after the pastoral needs of the students in the 16 to 18 age group. This role has helped me develop a range of skills complementary to my teaching. I have learnt to empathize with the students and have the ability to create an environment in which students feel safe to discuss their emotional needs. One of my main duties in this role is monitoring and tracking student progress through regular performance and predicted grades provided by their subject teachers. When reviewing progress I will discuss concerns with individuals, creating personalized learning programmes to support the student to 'get back on track'. I also understand the need for positive reinforcement where students are doing well and will ensure that I speak to all my students who are making good progress against their targets. In this pastoral role I believe that it is my responsibility to think of students and their learning holistically, respect them as individuals, encourage them to set challenging targets and support them in striving to meet their highest aspirations.

It is important for Heads of Year to lead their tutor team in developing a pastoral programme which suits the needs of the year group. This year I have developed modules for year 12 and year 13 tutorial programmes which the tutors have delivered. These modules were received positively by staff and students alike and have been important in ensuring that we offer a wide curriculum. To support this programme I have introduced an enrichment programme which includes the input of a range of outside speakers.

While my experience has been in a school sixth form environment I believe that the skills that I have developed, supported by my effective classroom management, will mean that I can apply these experiences to leading other year groups. Within my school I am a teacher governor which has given me an insight into the wider strategic leadership of the school and enables me to see how a role in middle leadership supports senior leaders.

The schools in my area have been involved in a fundraising project to build a school in the Gambia and last year I was privileged enough to lead the first group from my school in carrying out this work.

From the information I have gathered on your school, I can see that you are committed to providing the best education for the young people in your care and helping them to realize their ambitions through setting high aspirations. I am sure that my experience to date would enable me to hit the ground running and make a very positive contribution to your school as Head of Year and teacher of Design Technology.

Yours sincerely

Felicity Short

Interview questions
1. Why have you applied for this job?
I was really pleased when I saw the two advertisements at your school. This year I've been hoping that a Head of Year position would be advertised with my subject specialism available at the same time. I wasn't sure when I saw the advertisement if you would link the two positions but I decided the only way I would find out would be by applying.

I have been a teacher in this country for five years after having done a year's teaching in the Gambia when I first qualified. I love teaching Design Technology as it's great to see children who do not always have success in other areas of the curriculum have an opportunity to show their talents.

I decided that I would like to seek promotion but thought my skills were more suited to the pastoral side. Three years ago I took on the position of Assistant Head of Sixth Form at St Olave's and it has been fascinating to work with the older students and help them prepare for life after post-16 education. I would like to have a sole responsibility for a year group, so the position of Head of Year at your school would be an ideal chance for me to do this and help with your school's development.

Thoughts of the interviewer: *I hadn't originally planned to link these posts. It doesn't sound like she would take a sole DT post so it will be interesting to see what her Head of Year answers are like and whether she can relate her post-16 experience to pre-16 pupils.*

2. What is your perception of the pupils at this school?
It is so difficult to assess the pupils at any school and you make your judgements on a range of observations such as how the pupils were behaving as I drove to the school, the pupils who took me on a tour of a school and those in lessons and finally on the pupils at break and lunchtime.

Perhaps the most important thing is how the pupils appeared in lessons. On the whole they did seem on task and engaged in their learning though I did walk past a small group of year 8s in Geography where the teacher was struggling. The tour guides said that teacher was a supply teacher. The pupils who showed me around seemed proud of their school and liked most of their lessons but they did say that there was limited space for them at out of lessons.

The pupils out of lessons did seem a little lively but it was very windy today!

Thoughts of the interviewer: *She is either being kind or respectful as the pupils were very lively at lunch time and I know of at least one serious incident today. I'll pass on the Geography lesson comment. I would have liked a little more detail in this answer.*

3. How would you support a member of staff who was having difficulty with a class from your year group?
When I first became a teacher I had this assumption that the Head of Year would be able to solve problems with a difficult class and many teachers still hold this view, almost making the assumption that if there are difficult pupils it is the Head of Year's fault.

One thing that I have learnt is that teachers may need support in dealing with difficult pupils but the teacher must solve the problem, a Head of Year cannot make the children behave from distance.

If a teacher is having difficulty with a class, one of the first things I do is look at the group of pupils in the class. Sometimes by a pure chance a group has been formed with a set of pupils that shouldn't be taught together and any teacher would struggle with them. If that is the case it can be worth having a discussion with the curriculum leader to see if the grouping can be changed.

If this is not the case, I would then try to talk to the teacher to see what the problems were and see if we could discuss strategies that may make the situation better. I often find that seating plans can help teachers and it may be that I could assist in that process by helping the teacher with the seating plan and also to be present at the beginning of the lesson to help them with the organization.

I would discuss with the teacher the school's pupil management system and see if using this would help. Sometimes teachers can be reluctant to use these techniques as they see it as a mark of weakness but in reality it can be that the pupils do not take them seriously until they have done so.

There can be some rare occasions when the teacher is really struggling and I am surprised by the pupils involved. In this situation I would discuss the issues with a senior leader as it may be an issue with the teacher's competence.

Thoughts of the interviewer: *This is a strong answer recognizing her role in the process, understanding she cannot do it herself and being prepared to pass on information to the senior leadership team*

4. How important are assemblies to a Head of Year?
I have really enjoyed the opportunities I have had to deliver assemblies and it is a part of the job which I like. If you like and hopefully are good at giving assemblies they are a really important of the job. It is an opportunity to build your reputation with the year group as a whole and explain what you think is important on a week by week basis.

Sometimes as Head of Year you can feel that you are constantly telling a small group of children off and don't get the opportunity you would like to meet the good pupils. Assemblies can help here in two ways. First of all it means that you can give a positive message to the year group as a whole. It also means for me that it is a very visible reminder of all the hard working pupils in the year who are committed to the school and it shows that there is only a minority of other pupils.

I also think that assemblies should not just be something that only remains the ownership of the Head of Year. Assemblies can be really good opportunity for a tutor group to work together and perform to the rest of the year group, a chance for them to practise their public speaking or drama skills. It also gives other staff an opportunity to practise giving assemblies for their own personal development before they become a Head of Year or are asked to give whole school assemblies due to another promotion.

> Thoughts of the interviewer: *This is a clear explanation of the benefits of assemblies, it could have been even better if she had described an assembly she has done recently.*

5. What do you see as your biggest challenges in becoming a Head of Year at this school?

I think there are three big challenges for any teacher coming from outside the school to become a Head of Year, especially if you would like me to take over from another Head of Year. The first is that you have to have good classroom discipline so that all the pupils in your year group and other teachers in the school respect you. My classroom management has always been a strong part of my teaching skills and I would hope that the strategies that I have used with some very difficult groups at my current school will prove just as effective here.

The second challenge is getting to know all the pupils in the year group. The Head of Year is expected to be expert on the pupils in their group by staff and pupils alike. Sometimes when you join a new school you are advised to make your own judgements on the pupils as you teach them. However, for someone who is responsible for the pastoral care of a group of children I think it is very important to do your research and read the files of the pupils. One thing I would do if appointed is to ask different curriculum leaders for their experiences of children in my year as sometimes their performance in one subject area can be very different from their work elsewhere.

I think the third challenge is leading staff. One of the problems for many Heads of Year is that they are seen by staff as the person who solves their problems and even though they are classed as having a middle leader's role they do not actually lead any staff. The best Head of Year I worked for spent a lot of time working with his tutors and encouraging them to do as much pastoral work as possible. So when a pupil had been involved in an incident, rather than him stepping in to deal with the pupil he would instead often pass the incident on to the tutor to discuss with the pupil and follow up any sanction. The Head of Year would become involved when the issue became more serious or the incidents were more frequent. This gave the Head of Year more time to deal with the more difficult pupils but also empowered the tutors so they felt their role had more purpose. This is the style I would try to develop.

Thoughts of the interviewer: *Excellent answer both in terms of the content and the way she has structured the answer.*

6. How do you see the Head of Year's role in enrichment activities?
Often a key role of a Head of Year is to contact parents to discuss issues around their child either in person or by phone. Often the best time to do this at the end of the school day. One of the difficulties with this way of working is that it becomes difficult to run a regular after school activity.

I think one of the roles of a Head of Year with enrichment activity is to be available to help when extra staff are required so when the school production is taking place or different concerts, I think it is important for a Head of Year to help. This also gives an opportunity to see the pupils in a positive light and discover their talents. Another example would be to attend school discos that involve the year group, or trips which take place at the end of the school day.

I also think it is important to monitor the enrichment activities that the pupils participate in, to praise them if the PE department describe a good sporting occasion and to also encourage the pupils to take part in things if they have an interest in that area. There are some occasions when a Head of Year needs to encourage staff to run an activity if there is a demand from the year group or even look to bring in outside people if necessary.

On a personal level I think it is important not to forget my subject teaching. So in the spring term I have generally run extra-curricular sessions for students to finish their GCSE projects and I would want to continue with this.

Thoughts of the interviewer: *She is not really offering to do a regular extra-curricular session except for revision in the summer but explains clearly why. It is always useful to have staff who will do evening events like discos.*

7. Is there anything you'd like to ask us?
Even though I do have middle leadership experience from my role as assistant Head of Year, I think it is useful to have a good theoretical background. So I wondered if you would support me in doing the 'Leading from the middle' programme.

> Thoughts of the interviewer: *That sounds reasonable; we'll have to check how much it costs and how long she would be out of school.*

8. Do you feel the process has been fair?
Yes, I do and I've really enjoyed visiting school. It is such a positive place and I would really like the opportunity to work here. I am sure I could have a strong positive influence with your pupils.

9. Are you still a firm candidate for the job?
Yes!

Final thoughts

There is no doubt that the selection process for a middle leader is more demanding than that for a classroom teacher's role. You are constantly trying to demonstrate two things. The first is that you are a strong classroom practitioner and will get good results in the classroom as after all you will still spend around 80 per cent of your day teaching. The second is that you are trying to show the school that you can lead staff, that you can bring them together in working for a common purpose which is consistent with the vision of the senior leadership team.

Key points

1   Structure your letter to give examples of your teaching and your leadership potential.
2   Show the school that you are good teacher through your lesson and your interview knowledge.
3   Use good past observation judgements or validated results to add weight to your case.
4   Prepare examples of when you have led staff or run projects to discuss.
5   Look for opportunities to discuss how the school can be developed.

11 | Becoming a senior leader

The basics

There is a wide range of middle leadership roles and many teachers will have a number of middle leadership roles in their career. They may undertake curriculum roles such as being Head of a Department or a Faculty and may also move to pastoral roles such as Head of Year. Once you have attained one middle leadership role you may find that it is straightforward to move to another middle leadership role, whether in your own school or different one.

The next glass ceiling in terms of promotion is attaining a senior leadership role. In many schools there is a distinct division between senior leaders and other members of staff. The first obvious difference is that you will be on a different pay scale, the leadership scale. You will no longer get your upper pay spine payments and in some situations the pay for a senior leader in one school may be less than that for middle leader elsewhere. The pay for senior leaders is determined from the Headteacher's salary. The Headteacher's salary is driven by the size of the school. The Headteacher will be on a salary range and if performance is good, the Headteacher will move up this range. Other senior leaders will also have a range which must be the less than the Headteacher's. Again following satisfactory performance the senior leader can move up the scale.

There is a big difference between a senior leader's contracted hours of work and those of a middle leader. A middle leader is contracted to work 1265 hours of directed time whereas a senior leader does not have this, instead they are expected to work the reasonable instructions of their Headteacher. The most obvious impact of this is that most schools have senior leadership team meetings. In some schools these will occur in the school day, but at others it could be before school, after school or in the evening. There is a mystique about senior leadership team meetings at many schools and this is the meeting which often determines the development of the school and implementation of new initiatives.

Senior leaders are normally bound by a collective responsibility so even if you have disputed a policy during a senior leadership team meeting, if it has been agreed, you will be expected to put it into practice. There are some middle leaders who find this restrictive and hence do not wish to become a senior leader.

There is no doubt that many senior leaders will work longer hours than many other teachers as they will have their leadership tasks to complete and at the same time will teach a timetable and will be expected to be examples of good practice through their lessons and assessment procedures.

For many senior leaders it is the opportunity to develop strategic leadership which is the real pleasure in their role. The chance to develop a project which impacts upon the whole school and involves many teachers is a real challenge. It is this skill that schools will be looking for from potential senior leaders and hence you will need to demonstrate through your letter of application and the interview process.

This chapter looks at the applications of two leaders who are looking to gain a senior leader post. Jane is applying for a Deputy Head post in a primary school with the specific responsibility of SENCO for the school. Felicity is hoping to become a Director of Studies in an independent secondary school. This chapter presents their letters of application which are annotated to show strengths and weaknesses of their applications. Again a transcript of strong answers to interview questions is provided. All middle leaders who aspire to become senior leaders should practise the questions included and consider how their experiences should be applied to the type of school they are hoping to work in.

Identifying your starting point

- ◆ Why do you want to be a senior leader?
- ◆ What strategic projects have you been involved in?
- ◆ How do you explain these in your letter of application?
- ◆ What questions might an interviewer ask in relation to your letter?

The detail

Becoming a Deputy Head/SENCO of a primary school

Figure 11.1: Functional CV – senior leader

Jane Peacock
Personal profile

I have developed my leadership skills as a middle leader and through further study with the NCSL. This, coupled with my effective teaching at Key Stage 1, means that I am now ready to hold a senior leadership position focusing on inclusion.

Key achievements

◆ Implemented a coaching programme to develop the teaching of literacy to less able pupils in Key Stage 1.

◆ Evaluated the literacy curriculum in Key Stage 1 and Key Stage 2 and modified the early reception curriculum in the light of this.

◆ Led staff meetings on the primary languages strategy and ran a successful extra-curricular Spanish club.

◆ Dissertation on the links between children's drawing and their writing has been referenced in other academic works.

Education

2009–2010	National College for School Leadership Leadership Pathways
1996–2000	University of Plymouth BEd (Hons) Primary English with QTS Status Upper 2nd Class
1994–1996	The Grove Sixth Form A-levels: English (C), Spanish (C), Geography (D)

Employment history

2006–Present	St Christopher's Primary School Key Stage 1 Literacy Co-ordinator/Reception Teacher
2000–2006	Sir Francis Drake Primary School Key Stage 1 Teacher/Modern Foreign Language Co-ordinator

Interests

I read widely both fiction and non-fiction and enjoy writing my own unpublished fiction. I am a member of the Plymouth writer's guild which meets weekly. I also enjoy going to the theatre.

Figure 11.2: Letter of application – senior leader

Dear Mr Grant

It is with great pleasure and enthusiasm that I apply for this post in what presents itself as a vibrant and welcoming school. After my informative visit to you this afternoon, I am sure I would be happy as part of your team, and that I could fulfil the role of Deputy Head and SENCO with energy and professionalism. I share your commitment to giving children a caring education, and I especially admire the way your school welcomes and includes such a wide range of children.

I am currently the literacy co-ordinator and reception teacher of a small urban school with a significant number of children who have special education needs. The first year at school is so important in beginning to build the confidence of these children and trying to establish a routine that enables learning. Literacy is one of the major building blocks of learning and I consider it vital that children learn to love words and have a curiosity for the patterns that are created with them. Many of the children that I teach do not find a classroom environment straightforward and hence I am well versed in the challenges of dealing with pupils who have behavioural difficulties.

I feel strongly that schools thrive and rely on positive relationships and the development of these is an important aspect of a Deputy Head's role. It is people and relationships that are at the heart of our vocation and often a Deputy Head can be a key sounding board for both the staff and the Headteacher. I have built solid friendships with staff at my schools, sharing ideas and resources. After all, ten heads are always better than one! It is important to gain the respect of one's colleagues so that it is possible to coach and support them. Developing the skills of others is a key part of senior leadership and as literacy co-ordinator in my current school I have regularly led INSET sessions either to introduce new ideas or to facilitate the sharing of good practice already present in my school. We built on these sessions through the coaching group I led which specifically looked at teaching literacy to less able pupils.

I am a firm believer in the need for home–school relationships and have worked tirelessly to develop good links between home and school. This has involved regular communication through home–school books, making myself available to parents at the end of the school day, and producing a half-termly curriculum newsletter to inform them of the areas to be taught during the forthcoming half term. It is so important that a SENCO gains the trust of parents and I am sure these experiences will enable me to do this at St Christopher's.

As a Deputy Head and SENCO it is important to be able to prepare schemes of work which can be shared and used by others, rather than everybody being involved in duplication of resources. As literacy co-ordinator I reviewed the Key Stage 1 schemes of work and changed the reception ones in the light of this. I also worked with the other Key Stage 1 teachers to ensure there was a consistency of approach across the Key Stage.

In a small school it is important to recognize that there is a huge wealth of support available outside the school and in the realm of special educational needs it is possible to only meet some conditions once in career. In my current class I have a child who is a selective mute and I have sought advice from the local authority and then presented it to my colleagues. I always find it fascinating to work with outside agencies such as the Behaviour Support Team and educational psychologists.

In my last school, I held the position of Modern Foreign Languages (MFL) Co-ordinator. It was a very exciting time for Primary Languages, with their introduction into schools imminent. I spent time developing the scheme of work and had sole responsibility for implementing and teaching the subject across KS2. I relished the trust placed in me to deliver this new subject, and immensely enjoyed being a specialist in my school. Teaching the KS2 classes also afforded me contact with different children, and valuable experience of working with a wider age range. I was chosen by the local authority to help train the next cohort of MFL teachers, as the regional trainer for MFL had been impressed by my teaching during an informal observation. Part of my role as co-ordinator was to enthuse and motivate my colleagues in the area of language teaching. This saw me lead a staff meeting to inform KS2 teachers about the new Primary Languages Strategy and offer them support and ideas for their own teaching. I enjoyed fostering this confidence, and passing on my enthusiasm for the subject.

I have always had an interest in the written word whether it was using English or the challenge of trying to communicate in another language. As a student I studied emergent literacy skills for my degree dissertation. I researched the links between children's drawings and their knowledge of writing, and my work was referenced by an author in a book about children's drawings.

I am especially excited by this opportunity at your school, as I feel that after five years in my current post, I am ready for a new set of challenges. Although I would be new to the post of SENCO, I would love to learn and develop my abilities and knowledge, and I am confident that with a little support, I would blossom in this role. I think it's time for me to step up from being a great classroom teacher, and take on this new, very exciting leadership role.

I believe in a nurturing classroom where each child is respected and supported as an individual. I vow never to forget that it is the children who are at the heart of all I do – without an intrinsic love for them, their education would be poorer. I feel privileged to have had the education I have, and feel strongly that it is my duty to reciprocate this privilege, and enable more children each year to experience the joy that can be 'education'. As a Deputy Head and SENCO in your school, I believe that I can continue to turn these words into reality.

Yours sincerely

Jane Peacock

Interview questions
1. Why do you want to be a Deputy Head?
I have really enjoyed my two middle leadership roles of being MFL co-ordinator and literacy co-ordinator. I find it fascinating to work with other staff with the aim of improving the outcomes for a wider group of pupils than those who are in my class. I am now looking for the next challenge where I can work with a broader group of staff and have a positive impact on more pupils. I think the best way of doing this is to become a senior leader.

I am greatly interested in how a senior leader works with the Head to develop the strategic direction of the school and then how they work with the staff at the school so that everyone buys into the vision and works together to put this into practice. Being a Deputy Head will give me the opportunity to work with you to do this.

I am even more interested in this role because it also includes that of SENCO. I think at the heart of any successful school is how the least able member of its community is worked with so that they can first access and then benefit from the education before them. I also think it is important that the most able children are given the opportunity to excel.

I think that as Deputy Head and SENCO, I could help you in your aim of moving from Good to Outstanding and have the opportunity to develop my skills further too.

Thoughts of the interviewer: *She seems to be clear in her reasons for wishing to be Deputy Head and gives her key aim for the school..*

2. What are your perceptions of the staff of this school?
The staff have given me a very warm welcome this morning and your current Deputy Head has been particularly welcoming but it is also clear that she is held in considerable respect by the staff so I do not imagine her shoes will be easy to fill,

I think in small schools like this one staff relationships are so important and all the staff are dependent on each other. In small schools we cannot afford to carry a colleague. Everyone has to get involved and be committed to their own classroom and still take a role in the activities outside the classroom. From looking at your extra-curricular activities, it is clear that all your staff do this.

It's been really interesting to have time to walk around the classrooms and observe your teachers in action this morning and there is some really good practice from the teachers. I would say that all the teaching I saw was at least 'Good' in terms of Ofsted. However, one thing I did note was how hard the teachers were working especially with the junior pupils. I wondered at times whether the teachers or the pupils were working the hardest in the classrooms. Now I don't know if that was because there were strangers in the school and the teachers were over-compensating but I think in many schools there is a temptation for us to work harder and harder and as a result we don't always give the pupils enough space and they can feel dependent on us.

I think that the skills that I have developed in my previous school would be effective in working with your staff and I think that I would fit in, in the staffroom at this school.

> Thoughts of the interviewer: *Interesting idea that the staff are working harder than the pupils and she is probably correct. I am pleased that she has already seen filling my current Deputy's shoes will not be easy.*

3. What is your vision of an outstanding primary education?
At the heart of my vision for outstanding primary education is one word, nurturing. I think every child that we are lucky enough to teach has a unique set of talents and our role as a school and as an individual teacher is to identify those talents and then seek to nurture them. For some pupils it can be more difficult to find their talents than for others and I believe that means we have to search even harder for them.

Confidence and happiness are also central to a child's learning, so I also believe that we must nurture these aspects of a child's well-being if we wish their learning experience to be truly outstanding. For children who arrive at school from more challenging backgrounds or with some needs, it can be difficult to develop their confidence and in some ways this returns to the idea of finding their talents. If a child feels there is something that they do well, their confidence will be higher.

We need to provide opportunities both in and out of the classroom for children to develop their whole being so that they can use their talents to the full. Also by providing a supportive environment the children can really work on the aspects of school life that they may find difficult.

For education to be outstanding the teachers and other employees of the school must also give the very best experience to the children. I think this is a role for the leadership of a school to nurture their staff, to look for ways in which their practice can be improved and to tell them when they are doing a good job.

> Thoughts of the interviewer: *This is a very child-centred answer which I like but I would have hoped for some mention of the quality of teaching and learning or the attainment the pupils make.*

4. Tell me about a strategy that you have implemented in your school to help pupils with special educational needs?

Last year in Key Stage 1, we were concerned as to how effective our literacy teaching was in helping the least able children. I was convinced that all the teachers were good teachers but I wasn't sure how much our teaching built on the work of the teacher who had previously worked with those pupils.

Our aim was for us to share good practice in our literacy teaching and also build a common approach across Key Stage 1 which, while building on some of the ideas from the Literacy Strategy, was not dependent on it.

I asked the Head for permission to establish a coaching group among the Key Stage 1 team. On the September training day I led a session which suggested how teachers can coach each other and used the GROW model as a starting point. The six of us formed three coaching pairs for that year with the idea that in the second year we would swap pairs. We agreed that in each term we would each conduct a coaching observation with our partner. We used a combination of PPA time and the Head and Deputy agreed to cover our lessons for an hour, to facilitate the observations. Once a half term, the six of us had a formal meeting in an after school meeting slot where we shared our thoughts from our coaching observations.

After two terms of this project we felt much more confident that our teaching was building on previous practitioners' work. We also felt more of a KS1 team as we were spending time discussing the mechanics of teaching and learning rather than just exchanging schemes of work. In the summer term we fed back to KS2 teachers on our experience of our coaching project. They were very positive about the idea and this year rather than swapping KS1 partners, each KS1 teacher paired up with a KS2 teacher to form new coaching pairs. Each KS1 teacher then worked through the coaching model with their new partner. Rather than focusing on literacy for the less able we widened the focus to differentiation for the less able. This year we were really pleased as a school to obtain the inclusion quality mark and a major part of our evidence was our differentiation practice.

Thoughts of the interviewer: *She has structured this answer really well. I have a good understanding of what the aim of the project was, what she did and also what the school achieved. I also like the fact that this is a very team based response and not just what she has done.*

5. What do you think your role is in relation to me and also to the staff at the school?
I think the place of senior leaders in a primary school is fascinating. As primary senior leaders still have a heavy teaching commitment in smaller primaries, there is less of a division between teachers and senior leaders than there can be in larger schools. However, senior leaders in smaller primary schools still have to find the time to complete many senior leadership tasks after teaching while still finding the time and space to develop their school.

I think my role as Deputy in relation to you as Head is to act as a supporter and to be available to discuss how we can move the school forward. I hope that I would be able to take some of the burden from you so that you have a greater capacity for developing the school. I would hope that in private you would not mind me asking if there was an alternative way of doing something. However, I recognize that as the other senior leader in the school if you have decided on a course of action my role is then to present that to the staff and to always support you in front of the staff.

I would hope that over time I would be seen as a trusted colleague by the other staff and that if they had concerns they would be able to bring them to me so that I would be able to discuss them with you.

Finally if you are absent my role is to deputize for you and ensure the smooth running of the school. One Deputy always told me that as well doing what they thought was right they always asked a second question, is this what the Head would do? They needed to answer yes to both questions before they acted.

> Thoughts of the interviewer: *I am pleased that she realizes there is still heavy teaching commitment. She seems to have a good understanding of the relationship between Head and Deputy.*

6. How would you implement a new policy?
The key thing with any policy is that is should reflect the current working of the school and not be a bolt-on. So with any policy you have to consider what is being done in practice and work with the staff to implement and develop it so that it continues to reflect the school in operation.

This year I was asked to develop a new inclusion policy. My first task was to investigate the current policy and consider from that policy what we still did and to consider what additional work we now did. I made the amendments to the policy and then asked if I could present this to the Head and Deputy Head. We discussed the paper and they made some more amendments.

I then asked if I could have a meeting slot where I could present it to the whole staff. I split the staff up into three groups and also divided the policy into three sections so that each group could concentrate on one aspect of the policy and made any amendments. Each group then presented their thoughts and the rest of the staff could input at this stage. I tried to only act as a scribe at this point or to clarify information.

The next stage was to take the policy to the governors. The clerk to the governors sent this out in advance and I attended the governors' meeting to answer questions. They asked for a few amendments to be made which I then communicated to the staff. By the end of this process I felt that the inclusion policy did reflect the work of the school and that governors had a good understanding of the procedures that we have adopted.

Thoughts of the interviewer: *Other candidates have answered this theoretically. I like the way that she gives an answer with a solid example. She is aware that policies must have a practical basis and not just be a document for governors. This is also a well structured answer.*

7. *Is there anything you'd like to ask us?*
After answering your question on what my role is in relation to you, I'd be fascinated to know what you think my role is in relation to you and also what the chair of governors would consider my role is in relation to the governors.

Thoughts of the interviewer: *An interesting question! I've never been asked this before. It seems as though she is also assessing whether this is the right school for her.*

8. Are you still a firm candidate for the job?
Yes.

Becoming a Director of Studies of an independent secondary school

Figure 11.3: Functional CV – Director of Studies

Felicity Short
Personal profile
An innovative senior leader (enhanced by MEd studies) and outstanding teacher, with a commitment to individual pupils, whole school development, effective teaching and cultivating a diverse extra-curricular provision.

Key achievements
- Developed an academic tracking system to raise the level of attainment in the school.
- Re-wrote the school prospectus and managed recent open events.
- Rebuilt a faculty in crisis and then raised the GCSE results particularly in relation to A/A*.
- Three articles published in *Prep School* Magazine covering self-evaluation topics.

Education
2006–2010 The Open University
Masters in Education (Leadership and Management)
1993–1994 The University of Nottingham
PGCE (Secondary English)
1990–1993 Durham University
BA (Hons) English – 2nd Class
1998–1990 Queen Elizabeth's Grammar School
A-levels: English (A), History (A), German (B)

Employment history
2004–Present The Grove Independent School
Assistant Head and Head of English
1998–2004 Queen Mary's Grammar School
Second in English and Boarding Mistress
1994–1998 Long Pasture Technology College
Teacher of English

Interests
I have a love of literature, am a voracious reader and write on educational issues. I am a keen tennis player representing Grove Ladies.

Figure 11.4: Letter of application – Director of Studies

Dear Mr Johnston
I am writing in application for the post of Director of Studies as advertised on the Gabbitas website.

I have been most impressed both by the details received from Queen Mary's and the very favourable comments I have heard about the school from local educationalists. After working in three very different schools, I believe that small family independent schools with a rich variety of extra-curricular activities provide the ideal educational environment and I am most encouraged by the range of opportunities offered at Queen Mary's.

I believe that my experience of senior management and academic leadership, along with my work in transforming a faculty and excellent teaching, would enable me to fulfil this important role while providing me with the opportunities and challenges I am currently seeking. Academic study supports my practical skills and I have completed a Masters in Education (Leadership and Management). My wider reading ensures good understanding of educational issues and my current senior management role has given me both a whole school perspective and strategic leadership experience. I am now looking for an opportunity to develop these skills in a school where I can aim to build a curriculum that reflects the needs of individual pupils.

My personal attributes of dignity, confident communication skills and sense of humour, coupled with my enthusiasm for my subject and extra-curricular activities enable me to relate positively and constructively to my pupils – I possess a real passion for education and an ambition to make a difference for every young person with whom I work. I regularly contribute to educational debate by editing an in-house newsletter and have recently written a series of articles for *Prep School* magazine.

My recent work in tracking data analysis and the use of objective testing (YELLIS[1] and CATs data[2]) has enabled me to significantly raise the attainment and improve teaching and learning by focusing on the individual under-performing pupils. As a senior manager, I have practical experience of supporting staff by leading training and through performance management, lesson observation and work scrutiny.

High expectations, team work and interpersonal skills are a crucial element of leadership. When I took over my current post, the faculty had undergone a period of rapid staff change and lacked self-belief. Through collective efforts we worked to revise pupil expectations, introduced pupil targets, wrote new schemes of work and implemented various GCSE pathways for different pupils and after four terms the GCSE pass rate leapt considerably. We aim to stretch the most able and have increased the number of pupils who sit higher tier examinations. This ensures that pupils who nationally are in the top 15 per cent according to objective tests, achieve A/A* grades.

I am aware of the importance of school marketing particularly in relation to increasing the school roll. Due to staff absence I recently took on the task of re-writing the school prospectus, producing a marketing plan and managing the school open events which received very positive feedback. I have the energy to translate vision into reality through careful analysis and evaluation and I welcome opportunities to draw upon these wider skills in school.

My commitment as a teacher is to provide the highest quality of academic and pastoral care for pupils and my communication skills have enabled me to effectively manage disciplinary incidents, listening carefully to pupils, staff and parents and then responding in a calm but assertive manner. Outside the classroom, I lead whole school assemblies within

---

1 YELLIS (<u>YE</u>ar <u>11</u> <u>I</u>nformation <u>S</u>ystem) analyses the GCSE results of about 1300 schools, using its own tests in mathematics and vocabulary as a baseline from which to calculate value added. YELLIS tests are taken by students in years 10 or 11.
2 Cognitive Abilities Tests.

a Christian moral framework, enjoy coaching tennis and run popular journalism masterclasses.

My drive to succeed, fuelled by commitment to my colleagues and pupils, would make me a successful Director of Studies at Queen Mary's School. I would work tirelessly in supporting you as Headmaster, in implanting your vision for the school and I look forward to the opportunity to present myself at interview.

Yours sincerely

Felicity Short

Interview questions

1. Why do you want this job?

I have really enjoyed working as an Assistant Head and have found that I am particularly interested in the strategic leadership of a school with a focus on how the quality of teaching and learning can be developed in a school. I have worked at The Grove for seven years with five of them as Assistant Head. I now feel that it is the right time to look for the next promotion and the role of Director of Studies is the ideal one for me to develop my career and fully utilize the skills I have gathered so far.

I am happy at The Grove so I am looking to work in a specific type of school and that is why I was excited that a post at Queen Mary's has been advertised. I have heard of Queen Mary's good reputation from friends who live in the area. I also am very keen to continue to work in a small independent school as I feel this environment is the best for children's learning and development.

After having spent the morning at Queen Mary's I am impressed by what I have seen and from our conversations I feel that I could work well with you and learn from you. I also feel that I would be able to settle into the staff room and become a valued colleague.

Thoughts of the interviewer: *This answer seems consistent with the letter from the applicant but tells me little beyond. Why does he think it the right time for promotion?*

2. From looking around the school today what single change would you suggest making to raise attainment at the school?

One of the things I did before visiting the school was to study the GCSE examination results and see if there were any anomalies. One observation was the small numbers of children studying each of the three languages and I also noted that the results in German are significantly lower than the other languages. I was intrigued to see how languages are delivered in KS3 to prepare students for GCSE. As I understand, it all the children study French and German in year 7, in year 8 they also study Spanish and then in year 9 the pupils choose between Spanish and German but all continue to study French.

It is very challenging for the even the most able students to study three languages especially at the age of the 12. It is also noticeable how Spanish is much more popular at year 9 than German, I suppose because many children holiday in Spain. My suggestion would be for the children to all study French and Spanish through KS3. This means they have the time to develop these two languages. In year 9 for the most able pupils there could be the option for children to study German – perhaps they could opt for this to replace a design subject? The pupils should have stronger French and Spanish skills then to begin their GCSE.

For those pupils who drop their languages at KS3 we could use Asset Language or a GCSE short course to accredit the knowledge that they have learnt.

> Thoughts of the interviewer: *This is certainly a good idea and shows that she has analysed the data but there is no reference to anything she has seen in school today. Was there anything about the teaching and learning in the modern foreign languages?*

3. Talk me through how you have assessed the effectiveness of teaching and learning at your school?

When I became Assistant Head one of the first projects I worked on was our self-evaluation. At that stage there was no triangulation. Over the course of the year every member of staff was observed by a senior leader but this did not link into anything and did not build on previous observations.

I suggested that we should look at each department in turn: observe each member of staff within the department, conduct a book check and ask the Head of Department to write an analysis of the previous year's results.

We then had three sources of data from which to make judgements and we could also make suggestions for what the department should be working on next. The staff seemed more comfortable with this arrangement as they weren't being judged on one observation in isolation. In many cases we worked with the Heads of Departments to make the judgements so that then they could use this process as a lever to make a specific development within the department. The Head of Department was also reassured that the GCSE data was no longer looked at in isolation but instead a discussion took place and results were compared with our evaluation. This particularly pleased those Heads of Department who took a wider range of pupils in terms of ability.

> Thoughts of the interviewer: *This sounds a good process. I would be interested to know if they have made any improvements as a result. Were there any departments which had identified weaknesses?*

4. What actions would you take if you had identified a member of staff who was not performing effectively?

This is always a challenging situation but I do believe it is one that as senior leaders we should not shy away from. If it comes to my attention that a teacher is not performing, my first question is: is this a short-term issue? It could be a high performing member of staff has a family problem or is suffering from ill health and that their performance will soon return to their normal high levels.

If this is not the case and the member of staff seems stuck, I would try to establish what the issue is, by talking to them to see what they are finding difficult. I would look at the data from their GCSE classes and see what issues are shown. I would also have discreet conversations with their line manager.

If I conclude that there is a problem, then I would be looking to discuss it with you and find out what the school policy is on underperformance. It may be that through peer observation and support we could make improvement to the member of staff's practice. However, if this is not the case then we would have to discuss if competency needed to be looked at. After all the pupils only have one chance, parents are paying a considerable sum of money for their child's education and we should not be leaving them to experience a poor standard of teaching.

> Thoughts of the interviewer: *This is a well thought out, sensitive answer. I have two questions: at which point would she inform me; and has she ever been involved in this process as a senior leader?*

5. Tell me about a team you have developed? What strategies did you use?
Probably the best example of team building is when I first became Head of English. There was a married couple in the department who had emigrated at Christmas; one had been the Head of English. An aging member of the department had taken over as Head of Department but only lasted a term. The results had plummeted and, worst of all, the pupils had lost confidence in the department; I was appointed at Easter.

My vision was to ensure that the English Department was a strong team and the results were equal to those of Science and Maths.

In my first term I worked closely with the newly promoted second in department. We rewrote the schemes of work for KS4 and based this on a pathway model where the middle ability children had a choice of studying English Language and Literature or English Language and Media Studies. The least able pupils concentrated on English Language and also took functional skills tests. All the high ability children continued to study English Language and Literature. Another new teacher started in the second term. I ensured that I could support these relatively inexperienced members of staff and regularly popped in during the lessons.

The results rose at the end of the first year and in the second year when the pathways reached examination stage the English results were higher than both Maths and Science. In addition, when I was promoted my second in department became Head of Department and the newly qualified teacher became second in department. This has left the department on a firm footing.

> Thoughts of the interviewer: *She certainly seems very knowledgeable in how you change your curriculum and assessment to raise performance. I would like to know a little bit more about how she actually leads staff and creates a strong team. Does she believe in a collegiate approach or is she more direct?*

6. How do you think we could improve our marketing?
I think your prospectus is very strong. It is very professional and shows the school in a good light. A second main element of marketing is the open evening and if you wanted me to become involved with the school's marketing I would look very closely at this to see how we could improve it.

One of the key areas for an independent school is the area of so called first time buyers. These are parents who did not have an independent education themselves, but are considering it for their children. One strategy I have seen is where the nursery is rebranded so that it not known purely by the school name, so for example you could call your nursery 'Fox Hill Nursery at Queen Mary's'. The advantage of this is that lots of parents use nurseries while they work but may have discounted Queen Mary's thinking it is only a school. If the parents have a very good experience from the nursery they may choose to keep their pupils in the pre-prep.

A second idea is to look at how primary children could get a taste of the school informally. We could run a number of sports competitions and invite local primaries to take part, encouraging parents to collect their children by providing refreshments afterwards. This means that parents and children can have a look at the school and may then consider it.

I think with marketing, you have to always be trying to be creative, thinking 'what else can we do?' and not be prepared to settle for second best on the basis that 'we've always done it this way'.

> Thoughts of the interviewer: *I like the idea of the nursery renaming, that is a creative idea and one I'd be interested in discussing with her more.*

7. Is there anything you'd like to ask us?
As Director of Studies would I have an opportunity to involve myself in the work of the prep school?

> Thoughts of the interviewer: *I'm pleased she sees her role as wider than just the secondary school.*

8. Do you feel the process has been fair?
Yes.

9. Are you still a firm candidate for the job?
Yes!

Final thoughts

Not all teachers will wish to be a senior leader but for those who do, the recruitment process for this role can be the most challenging of any post. The selection process is likely to be long and arduous with a number of tasks over the days. Just as with any other position in a school, one of the keys is to prepare yourself fully by really considering what tasks have you done well in recent years and how they relate to whole school leadership. One of the mistakes many senior leader applicants make is to focus on departmental or Key Stage issues. Instead you must talk about whole school developments.

Being a senior leader can be a lonely role. It is important that you feel you will get along with other members of the senior team, especially the Head. If you do not feel this is the case, you may find the senior leadership post becomes very difficult.

Key points

1   Try to reach your own view of what strategic leadership is.
2   Carefully consider what successful initiatives you have led including their impact.
3   In your letter relate some of these initiatives to the job description of the post.
4   Practise answering questions which draw on these initiatives.
5   Try to get to know the Head and consider if this is an individual whom you feel you will get along with!

Section Three: Reflecting on Your Application and Interview

12 | Learning from feedback

The basics

Often when you attend an interview the school leader running the day will comment that they hope that you will enjoy the day. At which point there is often a nervous laugh from the candidates and a wry smile from the school leader. We all recognize that it is rare to enjoy the interview process; even if you get the job it will be likely that you endured a nerve-wracking and emotional day.

It is not really a question of enjoying the day; the most important thing is to see if you can learn from the experience. There is a whole range of ways in which your practice can improve as a result of applying for a job. These could be in your interview and application technique such as your written application, your lesson, how you approach a task or how you present yourself at interview. You may learn things about the type of school you wish to work in. The interview day may make you even more determined to work in that type of school or you may end the day re-thinking your previous plans. Finally you may be given ideas as to how you can make yourself a stronger candidate through your wider skills.

This third and final section of *Get That Teaching Job!* considers how you can reflect on the application and interview process and hopefully will enable you to find a positive in that depressing situation of not being successful at interview. This chapter looks at the feedback that you may receive from the school that you have applied for.

Identifying your starting point
- Did you get an interview?
- Would you like feedback on your application?
- Are you generally pleased with your interview performance?
- Has feedback been offered on your interview?

The detail

Feedback

Feedback is the most personal aspect of the job application process. There are no rules on the type of feedback given or even if feedback should be given. It was suggested earlier that few teachers are trained in how to organize an interview process; it is even truer that very few teachers are confident in giving feedback to applicants. They are likely to be nervous and worried about saying the wrong thing for a whole host of reasons from the legal to not wanting to reduce the confidence of an unsuccessful candidate further. Most interviewers are generally feeling very uncomfortable at this point anyway. Therefore most interviewers will want to get the feedback element over as quickly as possible and the advice they may give may not actually be that useful!

Feedback to written applications

If interviewers dislike giving feedback to unsuccessful candidates, they are likely to be even less keen on giving feedback to candidates who have not been shortlisted for interview. You may feel indignant that you spent all that time on an application but you have not been given an interview so the least that you deserve is some feedback on your letter. The likelihood is that a school leader may have read a whole host of letters so may not remember your letter in any detail. In addition, the process for shortlisting can be a very personal process. If you are determined to try to get some feedback on your letter of application, then the best way of approaching the situation is to send an email to the Headteacher asking if they can suggest any ways in which 'you can improve your application'. This is far less threatening than telephoning and asking for feedback. However, do not be surprised if none is forthcoming.

Where you may have more success in gaining feedback on a written application is if you apply for a job through a recruitment agency. Recruitment agencies wish to place good applications before employers so they may be willing to suggest improvements as you may apply to them again. In addition, they are likely to be more skilled in shortlisting applications. Some of the best advice I received was from a recruitment consultant. I was very lucky in catching her at the right time and as a result she was kind enough to spend time working on my application for me. After this advice I seemed to get an interview for nearly every job I applied for.

If you have good reputation with your current senior leadership team they may be prepared to give you advice, especially if you are looking for a promotion and they feel that you have worked hard for them. If you are a studying to be a teacher, your in-school mentor may give you advice but take care as they may not be that involved in the recruitment process so it may be better to see if a member of the senior leadership team will help you. You may also receive advice from your university tutor. The problem here is they are giving your entire tutor group the same advice and many of you may be applying in the same area. I once received eight applications from students from the same course for a teaching post and it was incredibly hard to shortlist them as their letter were so similar.

Feedback on interview performance

Most interviewers will offer you feedback after an interview if you have been unsuccessful. They may give you the choice of receiving it there and then or may offer to speak to you tomorrow. You need to judge the best time to hear the comments from an interviewer. You may decide that you want to get the process over with and wish to hear it straight away or you may wish to listen in a less emotional state the next day. One of the most important things is that you must try not to show any emotion or get angry – whatever you say will not change the interviewer's mind and it could confirm their opinion that they were right and if there are any future vacancies at this school you may have burnt your bridges.

You may find that some of the strangest comments that you will hear in teaching will be verbal feedback and you need to be ready to listen with a pinch of salt. Some of the most bizarre pieces of feedback I have heard have been around personal appearance. I was once told that I was too young for a senior leadership position and that I should grow a beard. One female candidate was also told that she was too young, should tie up her hair and not wear any make-up. A second female colleague was told that she was too pretty for senior leadership and to dye her blonde hair! Underlying those comments was the perception that all three candidates did not fit in with the school's perception of school leadership. For future interviews we all dressed as conservatively as we could and worked on our interview answers to suggest skills and experience beyond our years.

If you are attending an interview for a teaching position some of the most important feedback can be on how you approached the lesson. You may find that the type of lesson which generally receives good feedback in a challenging school receives very different feedback in a high achieving school. In the former the concentration may be on positive pupil engagement and the latter may be all around pupil progress. These are important comments to draw upon in future interview experiences.

You may also receive good feedback around a certain answer you gave. As a new teacher answers can sometimes be based on naïve optimism. I was once asked at interview about extra-curricular activities and I gave an extra long answer of all the sports that I could assist with. The Headteacher explained his concern that he was looking for Maths teacher and coaching in one sport would be a bonus. My answer had made him wonder if I actually wanted to teach Maths at all.

You will receive some feedback that can make you really cross because you do not agree with it and in this situation the best advice is to just listen and chalk it down to experience. You may also be cross to be given negative feedback about something in your application. One common comment is for potential NQTs to be told they did not get the job because they were not experienced enough. You can feel angry because the interviewer knew that before they interviewed you. However, you have to take the positive here – if that is the only reason they did not offer you the job you obviously interviewed well!

Some of the most illuminating feedback you can receive is from the external individuals who are invited by the school to give a particular viewpoint such as subject advisors or school improvement partners. They have no emotional involvement in the post and will often give the best advice. In addition if you are applying to a particular region they may meet or even interview you again. It is worth cultivating such individuals and listening carefully to their advice as they may be useful in the future.

Sometimes schools will not give you feedback or will just tell you that one candidate was better on the day. It may be incredibly frustrating after two days of interviews and the time in constructing an application but a school does have this right and even though it is hard, you just have to move on to the next one and take the positives of having got so close.

Final thoughts

Feedback can be useful to gauge your performance in an interview and there may be occasions when you receive some valuable comments which can help you in the future. However, if you feel that the feedback is not true and unhelpful, the best thing to do is ignore it. If it bothers you why not ask a trusted colleague at your school for their thoughts.

Key points

1   If you are looking for comments on your application, the best question is 'how can I improve my application?'
2   Try not to take feedback when you are feeling angry or upset.
3   Never argue with the person giving you feedback.
4   The best feedback is generally from external advisors.
5   Schools do not have to give you feedback.

13 | Making best use of supply work

The basics

Unfortunately for some teachers it will not matter how strong their application is, they will not be able to find a permanent job following graduation. This may be because you are limited by geography and there are not many jobs within commuting distance of your home. It may also be that there is a shortage of jobs for your subject, in your phase of education or in the specific type of school that you are targeting.

There will also be more experienced teachers who need to find supply work. Perhaps you had decided to make a career change which did not work out, you are exhausted by your current school and have handed in your notice before finding a job or you have been very unlucky in being made redundant.

At such times the obvious solution is to consider supply work, after all most of us need some income to pay the bills. There are two challenges with supply work. The first is either finding a supply position or obtaining supply work in the type of school that you wish to work in. The second is considering how you can use supply work to help build your career as well as keep a roof over your head.

This chapter looks at these two areas by considering what sort of supply work is available and also suggesting where you could look for a supply position.

Identifying your starting point
◆ How much supply work do you financially need?
◆ Have you got any existing contacts who may be able to help find you supply work?
◆ What kind of school would you like to work in?
◆ What length of contract would be best for you?

The detail

Duration of supply

The first decision that you need to make is what type of supply work you are looking for. This generally falls into two main groups. The first is temporary supply work when you work for short periods of time in a school and the second is when you have fixed term contract which could range from a month to an academic year.

Short-term supply work

In this situation you may work for odd days when a member of staff is out on course or a large number of teachers are ill on a particular day. This may be booked in advance or you may even be telephoned in the morning to see if you are available for school that day. You may also be booked for a period of days because a member of staff is ill, injured or perhaps on a residential trip.

In these situations you will typically find that the lessons are set. Your main tasks are to explain the lesson to the children, ensure they are behaving appropriately and that they are working. You do not have to undertake any marking nor will you be asked to attend parents' evenings. You have the opportunity to work in different schools or be very selective about the type of school that you wish to work in. There is the obvious disadvantage in that you do not have a regular source of income. It can also be stressful as the children in some schools can be very difficult for temporary supply teachers.

Fixed-term supply work

The second type of supply work is when you are placed on a fixed term contract of anything from half a term to an academic year. One of the most typical situations is where a member of staff is on maternity, paternity or even adopternity leave. It could be when a member of staff is on long-term sick leave or if a member of staff has resigned at short notice and the school has not been able to make a permanent appointment. In the current climate when schools are concerned as to future budgets, they may make one-year fixed-term contracts as they are unsure if they will be able to afford the post in a year's time.

In these situations you will be paid over the holidays but you will be expected to prepare lessons, mark the children's work and attend 1265-hour events such as parents' evenings. In this type of situation you obviously build up experience in one school. If you are a new teacher the school may be prepared to help you complete your NQT year. The obvious disadvantage is that you will only experience one school.

Contacting schools directly

If you are looking initially for short-term supply work, one good solution is to contact specific schools directly. In primary schools often the person to try to contact is the Headteacher. In large primary schools and most secondary schools there will be a range of people worth contacting. You may find it is the Deputy Head or another member of the senior leadership team who makes decisions on supply work and building a panel of supply teachers. Increasingly larger schools employ a member of the administration team to manage cover in a school.

It is often a good idea to telephone the school to ask who deals with supply staff. The individual may be reluctant to speak to you initially so it is good practice to send them an introductory email with a CV. This is one occasion when a CV is really valuable. If this is the type of school that you are especially keen to work in then you need to regularly follow up your introduction with emails to explain if you are still available. You may choose to do this fortnightly. Every school at some time has a cover crisis and it is likely that you will be asked to work in the school at some time.

You must see that first day of cover as an interview day. Schools will be looking to see that you are safe pair of hands and that you will follow the procedures that are explained to you, particularly in terms of administration such as attendance registers and with behavioural management systems. You need to show that you fit in, that you can set expectations for the children in line with a school ethos and that you won't cause huge problems for senior staff. However, if you do witness a major incident you must follow it up using the school systems.

If you are covering for one teacher, it is a good idea to leave brief notes about the lessons for that teacher. Try to write a balance of comments, no teacher wishes to return to a barrage of negative comments. It is also a good idea when you leave to try to have a brief conversation with a senior member of staff explaining your availability. However, too often supply staff spend too long talking to the Head or Deputy, and can then be seen as a drain and the school will be reluctant for them to return.

Using agencies

A second source of supply work is through the many supply agencies. You contact the supply agency of which you can find contact details via the internet, yellow pages or a teaching publication such as *TES*. You normally have a meeting with the agency and they will help you complete an application form and ensure that you have Criminal Records Bureau check completed. The advantage with an agency is that it is their job is to sell you to the school as they will only earn money from you when you are working. Typically you will work across a much wider range of schools but you can stipulate where you wish to work. In response to the many developments in safeguarding and child protection, some schools will only work through agencies as it is the agency's responsibility to complete these tasks. However, schools have to pay more for your services than if they employed you directly. For a list of agencies, see Chapter 2 (pages 23 to 28).

How can your career benefit from supply work?

It is amazing how many good members of staff use supply work as a springboard to a permanent position. I once did supply in school, was offered a full time post but rejected it as I'd found another job. A couple of years later I applied to that school for a middle leader post, even though inexperienced, and I was told that one of the reasons I got the job was that I was seen as a reliable classroom practitioner from my supply work and this enabled them to take the risk on my limited leadership experience.

I have appointed staff to the permanent positions after seeing them undertake supply work, on the basis that I've watched them be in almost a permanent interview for a period of time and I have so been so impressed that I have chosen not to spend the time or money in advertising!

If you are employed for short-term supply work, you will have the advantage of working in a range of schools. This may help you decide if there is a certain type of school that you wish to work in. As a PGCE student you may have only completed teaching practices in two schools so may not be aware of the many types of school that exist.

If you are to be an effective supply teacher you will have to develop strong and flexible classroom management techniques. What works in one school may not work in another. It is unlikely that you will have a relationship with the pupils so you will need to be very clear in your expectations and these skills will be very useful when you are in an interview observation lesson and when you do obtain a permanent post.

Most teachers recognize that the most effective method of ensuring pupils behave is by making lesson enjoyable and fun. As a supply teacher you may feel that you have to deliver the work that has been set. However, as you grow in confidence you may decide that you can teach the lesson topic in a more interesting way so you may have the opportunity to try things that you would not normally risk. If you are on short-term supply you must be quick on your feet to do this as you may only see the work set at the beginning of the day. One of the dangers of supply work is that you can fall into bad habits of just delivering lessons in the didactic manner in which most cover lessons are set.

As a supply teacher you must be prepared for the unexpected. The best supply teachers will carry a collection of resources with them in the case of work not being set or it not being able to be found. This can be an opportunity to design fail-safe lessons which work in the most difficult situations.

Final thoughts

Being a supply teacher can be very demanding and you can face challenging behaviour from pupils. What you must guard against is being stuck in a school where your confidence begins to ebb away. So if you feel that this is happening, you must be prepared to walk away from that school to find another position. That is easier to do than if you had accepted a permanent position in the school.

The more positive side of being a supply teacher is that you can work in a range of schools and have very different experiences. If you struggle in an interview situation or lack certain experiences you may find that this is a good way to prove yourself in the eyes of a school and hence find a permanent post. After all, what most schools are looking for are good teachers and they are always on the lookout for people with potential.

Key points

1   Spend time building relationship with schools and agencies.
2   Treat every supply day as an interview day.
3   Look to be seen as a safe pair of hands.
4   Try not to cause problems for senior leader but pass on major incidents.
5   Always thank the school for opportunity.

14 | The power of networking

The basics

While you are looking for a job one of the key challenges to overcome is to show interviewers that you are safe pair of hands, that you will be reliable and that you are a good teacher. In the past it was commonplace to go for an interview and find an internal candidate. For a main scale teaching post this could have been a PGCE student or someone on a fixed-term contract. For middle leadership posts and senior leadership posts it could have been a member of staff looking for promotion. I was once told by the Principal of a large and successful school that 80 per cent of the time he appointed internal candidates. I can remember thinking at the time that up against two internal candidates it would be unlikely I would get the job but I would do my best to make the interviewers think hard about their choice.

The reason that internal candidates often got jobs was that they were seen as dependable and the school was conscious that they were not taking a risk on a candidate that they may have only met for three or four hours.

It is obviously impossible to turn yourself into an internal candidate when you are not in the school but if the interviewers have some kind of connection with you above that of your application form you are beginning to create a similar type of feeling, albeit on a lower level than an interviewer has for internal candidate.

The mechanism to create this feeling is generally known as networking. If you pick up any business leadership book you can almost guarantee there will be a section on networking: the same would be true of lots of business guides to 'Getting the Perfect Job' and many coaching books. You might consider that networking is not necessary for teachers working in schools. A number of years ago I attended a seminar run by one of the teaching unions covering job search and one of the topics considered was networking. My first impression of such a session within the course was it was probably not much use. After all, weren't teaching jobs always advertised and isn't there an equal opportunities interview process, and anyway what were the chances of making a contact in a school that I wanted to work in? However, now I realize that networking is a very powerful tool in the job hunter's armoury.

Of course networking is not a quick fix; it takes time and commitment. If you decide to follow the advice in this chapter it may not help you get the job you are currently looking for but it may help you get your next job. I can always remember being offered a senior leadership post in a school which unfortunately I had to turn down as I could not afford to buy a house in the area at the time. I had often meant to keep in touch with the Principal of the College and explain how my career had progressed but never got round to it. I then saw a more senior position at his college which I applied for but was not shortlisted. I now think that if I had kept in touch I may have been interviewed for the post!

True networking is about far more than just looking for a job. This final chapter considers what networking is, how it can be useful and how you can go about building your networks to aid your work in school and hopefully as a sophisticated weapon in helping you get that job!

Identifying your starting point

◆   What do you think a network is?
◆   What contacts have you got in the type of school that you would like to work in?
◆   Do you regularly keep in touch with them?
◆   How can you build your network further?

The detail

What is a network?
In the context of school, your network is all the people you know who are related to education and your school. This could include a huge variety of people from those you studied with to colleagues you have met on interview. In business the definition, certainly in a sales environment, is far wider as it will include anyone that can be sold to. The careers website, Monster suggests the following people:

◆   old school, college or university classmates
◆   distant family members

- ◆ your friends' families
- ◆ your doctor, lawyer or accountant
- ◆ former colleagues or bosses
- ◆ club members or anyone else you meet socially.

I think it is this kind of list that can make educationalists feel that networking is not for them and not suitable in helping them with their role. Instead networks need to be fit for a certain purpose such as aiding you in your work in school and in the future hopefully help with job hunting.

How do I network?
There are probably three stages to networking. The first is making a new contact with someone. If you meet someone on a course with whom you would like to keep in contact you need to get their contact details; an email address perhaps, their school name and any other information. It is a good idea to keep some notes on the person. If you use Outlook at school it is relatively easy to use the notes section of the contact page to record information about them.

The second stage of networking is keeping in touch with the contact. Some people will actually set themselves some kind of target of touching base with a contact perhaps every term or every year. The world of email makes this easy. You can soon send a quick note asking how someone is, what their opinion is of a new innovation or send them an article or a piece of information that they may find interesting.

The third stage of networking may be when you ask them for help with a certain project you are working on. You may be considering buying a new scheme of work and ask contacts in your network who share that subject specialism if they have any experience of the scheme or if they would suggest something better. You may be working on a project for the first time such as the Key Stage 4 options process and ask senior leaders in your network if they would be prepared to share their systems with you. The reverse could also happen and the contact asks for your help!

Figure 14.1: The three stages to networking

Who is already in my network?

There can be many opportunities to build an education network if you are self-aware and are prepared. In effect everyone you meet through your job is a potential member of your network and you may meet some outside work too. The first category could be people with whom you have worked in the past and either they or you have moved on to new schools. If you go on a course the people you meet there are another group (and don't forget the trainer). What about colleagues in local schools? Why not contact local schools that you wish to work in and see if it is possible to view the school or department to help you? Always keep such meetings brief as it is very easy to outstay your welcome. You should get some ideas to help your teaching and if a job comes up at the school they hopefully remember you positively.

If you go to a job interview you could keep in touch with fellow candidates and see how they get on in the future. You never know you may attend an interview at their school and they may put in a good word or they may even be doing the interviewing! If you receive very positive feedback with the interviewers you need to include them in your network. They may have a similar vacancy and rather than advertising you may be lucky enough to receive a telephone call; this is a technique that I have used on occasion. Finally do not forget any local authority advisors who are present, as they often appear on the interview circuit, especially at senior leadership level.

You may be involved in Initial Teacher Training and the colleagues at the local university are potential members of your network. Don't forget other groups such as local authority officials.

Figure 14.2: Diagram showing who is already in my network?

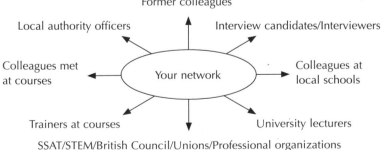

Former colleagues

Local authority officers

Interview candidates/Interviewers

Colleagues met at courses

Your network

Colleagues at local schools

Trainers at courses

University lecturers

SSAT/STEM/British Council/Unions/Professional organizations

Local authority officers are often very skilled as networking as this can be their calling card. One officer explained to me that networking 'lies at the heart of how we operate and the support we are able to offer to schools'. She facilitated a group of eight teachers and teaching assistants from special, secondary and primary phases, who met six times a year to reflect on their practice, share ideas and develop these in their own contexts. 'Networked approaches provide an invaluable opportunity to make connections with practitioners we would not normally get to "play" with and build relationships with them, underpinned by common and openly shared values', she explained.

Keeping contacts warm

With email it is so much easier to keep in touch with people and short regular emails are often nice to receive. It is important not to leave it too long between messages as when you go to someone for advice they may have forgotten you. Equally unless you are a friend, you do not want to bombard people with emails. Finally, do not be seen as a networker who only gets in touch when they want something; people are less likely to help someone with that reputation. In terms of job hunting you do not want your first contact to be when the school has a job advertised.

Can networking help career progression?

In industry regular statistics are released that suggest over half of all jobs are never advertised. Sometimes even higher percentages are quoted. As a result networking is even more important in industry as it is through networking that people may be aware of new opportunities and hence jobs may not be formally advertised.

In education this is less likely to be the case but it is surprising how useful networking can be to developing your career. Schools are always on the lookout for good staff, so if you have a contact at the right level in a school this may help your application to be shortlisted. All recruiters try to be as fair as possible but with lots of letters to study if a colleague says, 'Oh yes I know them, they always seem to be good' this can move your application onto the shortlisting pile.

As in any industry, people should not use networking to ask for a job. There are many methods where you can use networking to try to give you an advantage. If you have been for a job in a school which you really liked and were close to being appointed why not keep in contact with the interviewers and keep them informed of what you were working on or ask them for advice? If a school loses a member a staff close to deadline date they are often prepared to contact people who came close last time and see if they would still be interested.

If you meet a senior leader at a school that you would like to work in, you could ask them if they would be prepared to read through a draft application from you to give advice on its content. It may keep you in mind and they think of you when they are advertising a post.

In teaching when you only have one chance to apply for a job and time is short, it can be good practice to ask other contacts if they will give you advice on their application. However, if it is the first time you have been in touch with that contact they may not be as receptive as if you'd been in regular contact.

Final thoughts

The art of networking for career progression is playing a long game. The contacts that you are making now may not bear fruition for another five years. However, there is no doubt that networking can be very useful.

There can be times when you are job hunting but there are no suitable jobs advertised and you can feel that there is nothing you can do to move your career along. This is an ideal time for you to keep up to date with your contacts and, who knows, they may have opportunities for you just around the corner.

Key points

1 Keep a record of your contacts.
2 Ensure you that your contacts are kept warm with regular updates.
3 When you meet new people make an effort to find an email address.
4 Don't leave it until a job is advertised before you make contact.

Index